Does
TRAINING
Work For
DISPLACED
WORKERS?

A
Survey
of
Existing
Evidence

Duane E. Leigh
Washington State University

HD
5715.2
.L45
1990

1990

W. E. UPJOHN INSTITUTE for Employment Research
Kalamazoo, Michigan

Library of Congress Cataloging-in-Publication Data

Leigh, Duane E.
    Does training work for displaced workers? : a survey of existing
evidence / Duane E. Leigh.
      p.   cm.
    Includes bibliographical references and index.
    ISBN 0-88099-093-7 (hardcover : acid-free). — ISBN 0-88099-094-5
(paper : acid-free)
    1. Occupational retraining—United States.   I. Title.
HD5715.2.L45   1990
331.25'924'0973—dc20   ∞   90-38433
                                                                  CIP

THE INSTITUTE, a nonprofit research organization, was established on July 1, 1945. It is an activity of the W. E. Upjohn Unemployment Trustee Corporation, which was formed in 1932 to administer a fund set aside by the late Dr. W. E. Upjohn for the purpose of carrying on "research into the causes and effects of unemployment and measures for the alleviation of unemployment."

The Author

Duane E. Leigh is a professor of economics at Washington State University, Pullman, Washington. He earned his Ph.D. in economics from Michigan State University in 1969, and he has held teaching and research appointments at the University of Wisconsin–Madison and the University of Virginia. In addition to his work on training programs and displaced workers, he has published articles relating to racial differences in unemployment and labor force participation rates, factors leading to occupational advancement, union effects on wage and nonwage forms of worker compensation, and the determination of workers' preferences for union membership. He is also the author of two previous monographs—*An Analysis of the Determinants of Occupational Upgrading* and *Assisting Displaced Workers: Do the States Have a Better Idea?* The latter was published by the Upjohn Institute in 1989.

Acknowledgments

This monograph is a revised and expanded version of a report submitted in July 1989 to the Bureau of International Labor Affairs (ILAB) of the U.S. Department of Labor. The financial support of ILAB is gratefully acknowledged as well as the guidance and encouragement of Robert Bednarzik of the ILAB staff who served as my project monitor. Additional financial support supplied by the Upjohn Institute is also much appreciated.

The following individuals furnished me with very helpful comments on one or more chapters of various drafts of the manuscript:

John Addison	University of South Carolina
Scott Cardell	Washington State University
Richard Curtain	Department of Employment, Education and Training, Australia
David Stambrook	Employment and Immigration Canada
Ernst Stromsdorfer	Washington State University

In addition, Robert Cook of Micro Systems, Inc. read and commented on the entire draft that was submitted to the Upjohn Institute. Finally, David Gillette provided able research assistance, and Judy Gentry expeditiously handled the final steps of preparing the manuscript for publication.

Policy Summary

Displaced workers are usually defined as persons on layoff with a stable employment history who have little chance of being recalled to jobs with their old employer or even in their old industry. The need to seek reemployment in a new occupation or industry sometimes requires that displaced workers acquire the vocational skills needed in expanding industries, and may also require the enhancement of long-forgotten job search skills. Retraining is broadly defined to include both.

As stated by the author, the principal roles for publicly sponsored retraining programs are twofold: (1) to reduce the private and social costs associated with unnecessary delays in the reemployment process, and (2) to assist in the replacement of specific human capital lost when a permanent layoff takes place. This study examines nine different demonstration projects and operating programs to determine how well public retraining programs for displaced workers fulfill these roles.

The book attempts to answer four policy questions regarding the effectiveness of retraining programs in speeding up the reemployment of workers displaced from jobs by permanent layoffs or plant closures:

- Do some types of training work better than others?
- Do some groups of workers benefit more from training than others?
- To the extent that training improves reemployment prospects, does it work by increasing post-training wage rates or by reducing the duration of unemployment?
- Referring specifically to vocational training, how do we know what to train workers to do?

One unambiguous finding of the study is that job search assistance strongly affects a variety of labor market outcomes, including earnings, placement and employment rates, and level of UI benefits. Given its cost effectiveness, the evidence analyzed in this study suggests that job search assistance should be the core of any adjustment assistance services offered displaced workers. With respect to other services, however, the evidence is not as conclusive. There is no clear evidence that either classroom or on-the-job training has a significant net impact on employment or earnings. The author proposes an agenda for future research, including the collection of additional evidence on the determinants of success or failure of training programs.

Contents

Tables

1
Introduction

For more than 25 years the federal government and individual state governments have provided retraining programs to ease the labor market adjustments required of workers directly or indirectly displaced from their jobs by a mass layoff or plant closure. Displaced workers are usually defined as persons on layoff who possess a stable employment history. In addition to their work experience, the main distinction between displaced and other laid-off workers is that the displaced have little chance of being recalled to jobs with their old employer or even in their old industry. Displaced workers are therefore said to be "permanently" laid off.

The report of the Secretary of Labor's Task Force on Economic Adjustment and Worker Dislocation (1986: 13–16) presents a useful capsule description of the characteristics of displaced workers. Drawing on the information available for individual displaced workers in the 1984 and 1986 Displaced Worker Surveys (DWS), the report points out that almost 50 percent of displaced workers had lost jobs in manufacturing, mostly in durable goods manufacturing industries such as primary metals and transportation equipment. Only 20 percent of all employed workers and about 23 percent of all unemployed workers, in contrast, are associated with manufacturing. In addition, the displaced were disproportionately blue-collar workers concentrated in the Midwest and other sections of the country with a heavy manufacturing base.

As compared to the workforce as a whole, the Task Force report also notes that displaced workers endure significantly longer spells of unemployment following layoff. In particular, there is a much smaller fraction of the displaced in the 1- to 4-week unemployment duration category and a much larger fraction in the 15- to 26-week category. Because layoffs tend to be permanent rather than temporary, moreover, occupational mobility is higher for displaced workers than for other workers. About one-half of those displaced workers reemployed as of January 1984 had made a major occupational change. Using 1984 DWS data, Flaim and Sehgal (1985) also point out that about 30 percent of displaced workers reemployed in full-time wage and salary jobs suffered an earnings loss of 20 percent or more and that nearly one-quarter of reemployed displaced workers failed to regain the group health insurance coverage they enjoyed on their lost job. Not to be overlooked, finally, are the severe emotional adjustments required of workers abruptly displaced from jobs they perceived as "good jobs" and expected to retain into the foreseeable future.

The need to seek reemployment in a new occupation or industry may require that displaced workers tool up in the vocational skills required to qualify for jobs in expanding industries. A stable work history suggests, moreover, that the job search skills of many displaced workers are likely to have grown rusty from disuse because of a lengthy attachment to the pre-layoff employer. For the second of these reasons, retraining is defined broadly to include the enhancement of job search skills in addition to the traditional focus on vocational training. The principal roles for publicly sponsored retraining programs are twofold: (1) to reduce the private and social costs associated with unnecessary delays in the reemployment process, and (2) to assist in the replacement of specific human capital lost when a permanent layoff unexpectedly takes place.

Questions to be Answered

The purpose of this monograph is to answer the following research questions involving government training assistance to displaced workers:

1. Do some types of training work better than others?

2. Do some groups of workers benefit more from training than others?

3. To the extent that training improves reemployment prospects, does it work by increasing post-training wage rates or by reducing the duration of unemployment?

4. Referring specifically to vocational training, how do we know what to train workers to do?

Question 1 raises the possibility that the major types of training—classroom training (CT), on-the-job training (OJT), job search assistance (JSA), and remedial education—may differ in the benefits they offer displaced workers, as well as in their costs. The premise of CT is that the specific skills of displaced workers have been made largely obsolete, but that skills of potential interest to a number of employers can be developed through intensive, formal training in a classroom setting. OJT, on the other hand, is appropriate in the acquisition of firm-specific skills that can most efficiently be learned on the job. The objective of JSA is basically to assist job-ready workers to develop effective job-seeking skills. Finally, remedial education programs are designed to assist the perhaps 20 percent of displaced workers who have a deficiency in reading or problem solving skills severe enough to retard reemployment or even the acquisition of new job skills.

Question 2 is posed in recognition of the fact that not all displaced workers may benefit equally from retraining services and, moreover, that not all of these workers are equally in need of adjustment assistance. The analysis of 1984 DWS data by Podgursky and Swaim (1987a) shows that the distribution of completed spells of joblessness is highly skewed to the right. While nearly half of the respondents in their sample found jobs within 14 weeks of displacement, a substantial minority faced a high risk of being jobless for a year or more. It is this minority to whom adjustment assistance efforts should be targeted. Podgursky and Swaim loosely identify these individuals to include workers displaced from blue-collar occupations, workers with below-average levels of education, racial minorities and women, and residents of communities with above-average unemployment rates. In a parallel paper also using DWS data, Podgursky and Swaim (1987b) report that a sizable minority of displaced workers—mostly workers with substantial specific human capital investments—experienced large and enduring earnings losses upon reemployment.

The distinction made in Question 3 is intended to separate the effect of vocational training on labor productivity as measured by a higher post-training hourly wage from its effect in speeding up reemployment by providing a credential that moves workers up in the queue for vacant jobs. Question 4, finally, focuses attention on the issue of how to identify growth occupations and develop appropriate curricula so that successful program graduates have a reasonable chance of being hired and retained in training-related jobs.

The policy relevance of these research questions is brought out clearly in the provisions of the Economic Dislocation and Worker Adjustment Assistance Act (EDWAA) passed by Congress and signed into law by President Reagan in August 1988. This act amended the existing Title III of the Job Training Partnership Act (JTPA), and sharply increased the level of federal funds to be used by the states in establishing programs to meet the adjustment assistance needs of displaced workers. Program services, many of which were recommended by the Secretary of Labor's Task Force report (1986), are described in the enabling legislation under the headings of "basic readjustment services" and "retraining services." Basic readjustment services are defined to include such JSA services as outreach and orientation, job and career counseling, testing and assessment, provision of labor market information, job clubs, job development, and supportive services such as child care and commuting assistance. In addition to CT and OJT programs and remedial education, retraining services include relocation allowances, literacy and English programs for non-English speakers, and entrepreneurial training. The act also specifies that funds are not to be spent on public service employment (PSE) programs, but that needs-related payments may be provided to an eligible displaced worker who does not qualify or has ceased to qualify for unemployment compensation in order that he or she may participate in training or education programs.

EDWAA thus allows a great deal of latitude in the types of displaced worker programs eligible for federal funding. It is my intention that the answers to the four research questions posed in this chapter will be of assistance to state and federal government officials charged with the responsibilities of designing, implementing, operating, and monitoring the displaced worker programs called for by the new legislation.

Organization of the Study

The monograph begins in chapter 2 with an overview of the existing evaluations of federally funded Comprehensive Employment and Training Act (CETA) programs. CETA predated JTPA and provided funding for training and PSE programs during the 1973–82 period. Although CETA programs were not limited to training assistance or to serving displaced workers, the CETA evaluations are a good starting point for two reasons. First, they provide baseline quantitative estimates to which the impacts of later programs and demonstration projects can be compared. Second and more important, a discussion of the CETA evaluations represents an opportunity to introduce some of the main methodological issues involved in program evaluation.

Chapter 3 is in many respects the heart of the monograph. Here the large volume of quantitative evidence generated by four major demonstration projects funded by the federal government during the 1980s is examined in detail. These projects are the Downriver program, the Buffalo program of the Dislocated Worker Demonstration Project, the Texas Worker Adjustment Demonstration (WAD), and the New Jersey Unemployment Insurance (UI) Reemployment Demonstration project.

Chapter 4 follows with an analysis of the largely qualitative evidence on the design and implementation of statewide continuing programs in California and Minnesota. California's Employment Training Panel (ETP) provides classroom training to displaced workers and employed workers at risk of displacement, while the Minnesota Employment and Economic Development (MEED) program is targeted wage-subsidy initiative. Considered also in connection with the Minnesota program are results from the federally funded Dayton targeted wage-subsidy experiment. This chapter is particularly helpful in providing insight into Question 4.

In chapters 5 and 6, the discussion moves from domestic retraining programs to a consideration of programs provided displaced workers by other nations. Examined in chapter 5 are the training programs presently in place in Canada and the available quantitative evaluations of the National Institutional Training Program

(NITP) and the Canadian Manpower Industrial Training Program (CMITP). Similarly, chapter 6 discusses Australia's federally funded displaced worker programs and presents the main results of an evaluation of the Labour Adjustment Training Arrangements (LATA) program.

Chapter 7 concludes the monograph with answers to the four policy questions and an agenda for future research.

2
CETA Evaluations

The federal government's first comprehensive attempt to provide adjustment assistance to displaced workers was the Manpower Development and Training Act (MDTA). Passed in 1962, MDTA represented the response of Congress to a rising national unemployment rate coupled with growing concern over the effects of technological change on the employment options of mid-career adult workers.[1] The primary objective of the program was to provide retraining for workers whose skills had been made obsolete by new technology. By the mid-1960s, however, an improved labor market and lessened concern over automation led to a shift in interest and funding away from the reemployment problems of displaced workers and toward the employability of disadvantaged young people and welfare recipients.

The next major federal training initiative was the passage in 1973 of CETA, which consolidated nine earlier programs including MDTA. Program services funded under CETA were directed toward workers unemployed for both structural and cyclical reasons, and program participants typically received income-maintenance stipends. The range of services provided during CETA's 10-year existence included classroom training, on-the-job training in the private sector, PSE, and work experience (subsidized public-sector jobs emphasizing work habits and basic skill development designed for individuals with essentially no prior labor market experience). A small number of participants also received job placement services (called "direct referrals"). As unemployment rose during the 1970s, CETA expenditures shifted away from training programs toward the provision of PSE job slots. PSE programs typically provided little or no training. By 1981, charges of careless management and enrollment of ineligible applicants led to the elimination of CETA funding for PSE jobs, and CETA itself was not renewed at its scheduled 1982 expiration data.[2]

Methodological Approaches

A number of evaluation studies of MDTA programs appeared in the late 1960s and early 1970s, but these early attempts at evaluation were generally hampered by the lack of a comparison or control group, as well as the absence of good information on earnings.[3] The fundamental problem in program evaluation is developing a reliable methodology for assessing what would have happened to participants had they not enrolled in the program. Without a comparison or control group, analysts interested in obtaining net impact estimates are basically limited to using participants as their own control group by comparing post-program labor market outcomes like earnings with the level of participants' own pre-program earnings. Referring to the taxonomy in table 2.1, this is the first of the four methodological approaches used in the evaluation reports described in this study. The major difficulty with the pre-program/post-program approach is that the pre-program dip in earnings that caused workers to seek to enroll in the program in the first place may be merely a temporary interruption in their permanent time path of earnings. If the pre-program dip is caused by some transitory labor market phenomenon, the program would receive "credit" for a rebound in earnings that would have happened anyway. In addition, all other events that are time conditional (e.g., an upturn in the economy) are assumed constant—an assumption which is patently false.

The second methodological approach described in table 2.1 involves constructing a comparison group from data on program-eligible workers who did not, for whatever reason, participate in the program. This methodology has the advantage of making it unnecessary to control statistically for differences between members of the treatment and comparison groups since they are drawn from the same population. It has the important disadvantage, however, of bringing to the forefront the problem of "selection bias." This problem arises because program participants both choose to enroll and are selected by program operators. Thus, personal characteristics such as ability and motivation that are unobservable to the analyst are likely to lead to a positive correlation between program participation and the error term in the earnings equation. In other words, a

Table 2.1
Taxonomy of Methodological Approaches to Estimating
Net Program Impacts

Methodological approach	Discussion	Programs and demonstrations examined
Pre-program/ post-program comparison	Earnings of participants are likely to recover from their "pre-program dip" even in the absence of the program. Hence, the effect of the program will be overstated.	California's ETP and Canada's CMITP
Use of a self-selected comparison group composed of nonparticipants from the program-eligible population	Has the advantage that participants and comparison group members are drawn from the same population, but the disadvantage of the "selection bias" that results if participants would have had different earnings than nonparticipants, even in the absence of the program.	Canada's NITP and Australia's LATA
Use of an external comparison group	Since participants and nonparticipants are not drawn from the same population, it is necessary to control statistically for differences between participants and comparison group members. This is accomplished by (1) specifying an earnings function that would prevail for both groups in the absence of the program (which may also include observable determinants of the participation decision) and/or (2) selecting a "matched" subsample that has approximately the same characteristics on average as the participant sample.	CETA, Downriver, and Buffalo nontarget-plant sample
Use of a randomly selected control group from the program-eligible population	By randomly assigning participants and nonparticipants, selection bias is avoided by directly breaking the link between participation and unobservable determinants of earnings.	Buffalo target-plant sample, Texas' WAD, the New Jersey UI demonstration, and the Dayton wage-subsidy experiment

selection bias arises because the earnings of program graduates would differ from the earnings of nonparticipants, even in the absence of the program.

Although a few of the programs examined in this study have been evaluated using either the pre-program/post-program approach or a self-selected nonparticipant comparison group, most of the evaluations considered provide net impact estimates based on either an externally selected comparison group or a randomly selected control group drawn from the program-eligible population. An important feature of CETA was that, for the first time, the U.S. Department of Labor (USDOL) funded the development of a data base specifically designed for program evaluation. Termed the Continuous Longitudinal Manpower Survey (CLMS), this data base includes three components: (1) data for random samples of CETA enrollees collected quarterly beginning in 1975, (2) data for comparison groups drawn from March Current Population Survey (CPS) files, and (3) Social Security earnings records for each CETA enrollee and each member of the CPS comparison groups. Thus, the methodological approach to program evaluation permitted by CLMS data involves the use of an externally selected comparison group—in this case, a sample drawn from the CPS. As noted in table 2.1, a general problem with this third methodology is that differences between the treatment and comparison groups will exist because they are not drawn from the same population. The two groups are therefore not statistically equivalent. In the particular case of CLMS data, CETA eligibility was generally restricted to individuals in low-income families, with the result that CETA enrollees differ from members of the nationally representative CPS sample in terms of such characteristics as previous work experience and education.

The important advantage of the fourth methodological approach—that involving random assignment of program-eligible workers to treatment and control groups—is that the link is broken between program participation and unobservable determinants of earnings. This allows unbiased net program effects to be obtained. Most analysts therefore conclude that randomized experiments are necessary to produce reliable estimates of program impacts (see, for example, Fraker and Maynard 1987; and LaLond 1986). In defending the value of nonexperimental methods of program evaluation, however, Heckman, Hotz, and Dabos (1987: 421–24) emphasize the costs and practical difficulties of conducting social experiments and, in their view, the limited value of experimental data. They note, in particular, that participation in a training program entails a multistage process of application, selection, continuation in the program until completion, and job placement. An experimental assessment of the effect of training conditional on completing each stage of the process requires random assignment of each stage—something that is rarely done in social experiments. Hence, a case can be made that nonexperimental methods have a role to play in realistic plans of program evaluation.

Evaluation Results

Barnow (1987) provides a useful survey of 11 major CETA evaluations. Table 2.2 summarizes the net impact estimates presented in the five studies he surveyed that use data for adult workers and that provide some breakdown in the results by sex, race, and type of program service. Also shown are results from a recent CETA evaluation by Finifter (1987). The estimates measure the impact of CETA on the first year of post-program earnings for participants enrolled in 1975 and/or 1976 net of the earnings of the CPS comparison group. Since PSE and work experience offered enrollees relatively little training, the table focuses on training opportunities supplied through classroom and on-the-job training.

Three conclusions appear to be warranted. First, most of the estimates shown in the table for women are larger than those for men, with the male estimates often being zero or even negative. Bloom and McLaughlin (1982) suggest in this connection that regardless of program activity, the main effect of CETA training was to facilitate labor market entry. Thus, persons who were out of the labor market, primarily women, enjoyed a larger program impact than those with extensive but unsuccessful labor market experience, primarily men. If Bloom and McLaughlin's suggestion is correct, however, the net impact estimates for women will be upwardly biased to the extent that female labor force entrants are not a random sample of all women.

The second conclusion is that on-the-job training is typically more effective than classroom training, particularly for minority enrollees. The larger impact for OJT than CT is to be expected since the most job-ready of enrollees are those likely to be selected by employers for OJT slots. Relative to classroom training, OJT may also have a larger impact on earnings in the short run than in the long run be-

Table 2.2
Estimated CETA Net Impacts on Earnings of Adult Workers,
by Sex and Race

	Men		Women	
Study	**White**	**Minority**	**White**	**Minority**
Westat (1981)				
CT	$400	$ 200	$550	$ 500
OJT	750	1,150	550	1,200
Overall	200	200	500	600
Bassi (1983)				
CT	—	582–773	63–205	426–633
OJT	—	2,053–2,057	80–382	1,368–1,549
Overall	—	117–211	740–778	426–671
Bloom & McLaughlin (1982)				
CT	300	300	1,300	1,100
OJT	−200	1,500	1,200	800
Overall	200		800–1,300	
Dickinson, Johnson & West (1986)				
CT		−343		0
OJT		−363		35
Overall		−690		13
Geraci (1984)				
CT		372		1,201
OJT		612		882
Overall		—		—
Finifter (1987)				
CT		−9		507
OJT		686		723
Overall		—		—

Sources: Barnow (1987: table 3) for the Westat through Geraci studies, and Finifter (1987: table 1).

Note: "Overall" refers to the combined impact of CT, OJT, PSE, work experience, and multiple activities. — indicates that an estimate is not reported.

cause job retention is usually assured for a short time after the subsidy period ends.

Finally, the range of CETA net impact estimates shown in table 2.2 is uncomfortably wide. At first glance it may seem odd that studies using the same data set to estimate the same treatment effect should arrive at such different estimates. The basic problem is that the absence of a classical experiment in which sample members are randomly assigned to either the treatment group or the control group requires CLMS users to make a number of critical decisions. Most of these decisions involve (1) controlling for differences between members of the treatment and comparison groups, and (2) coping with the selection bias problem. With respect to the first issue, analysts of CLMS data have proceeded by specifying an earnings function that would prevail for both groups in the absence of the program and/or selecting a subsample of CPS respondents that matches CETA participants on a number of key variables determining earnings. The purpose of drawing a matched comparison sample is to reduce pre-program differences between the CETA and CPS samples so that the regression estimates will be less sensitive to the incorrect specification of the post-program earnings function. Weighting the observations in the earnings regression is also used to make mean values of the explanatory variables more alike in the treatment and comparison groups.

The seriousness of the selection bias problem appears to be reduced in CETA evaluations because the comparison group is drawn from CPS data rather than from the self-selected population of program-eligible nonparticipants. Nevertheless, program participation is not a random event; participants must have passed through a multistage screening process. Analysts of CLMS data have therefore pursued a number of different approaches in attempting to deal with the selection bias problem. In increasing order of complexity, these include (1) specifying additional explanatory variables in the post-program earnings equation to capture factors believed to be important in the selection process, (2) making specific assumptions about unobservable variables invariant over time which potentially affect both program selection and earnings in an attempt (typically using a first-difference estimator) to eliminate correlation in the earnings equation between the error term and the training variable, and (3) explicitly modeling the selection process in a separate participation equation and then jointly estimating the participation and earnings equations. The results reported by different analysts may clearly vary in important respects depending on the specification of the earnings function, the matching technique used, the attempt, if any, to model the selection procedure, the assumptions made about unobservable variables, and the decision reached on whether and how to weight CPS observations.

The multiplicity of decisions required of CLMS users makes it difficult to assess the extent to which differences in methodological approach account for the wide range of net impact estimates displayed in table 2.2. Fortunately, Dickinson, Johnson, and West (1986) perform the useful service of trying to reconcile their very low and even, for men, negative impact estimates with the sizable positive estimates reported for both men and women in the influential study by Westat (1981). Their analysis suggests that Westat's results are quite sensitive to (1) the omission of pre-enrollment earnings in the post-program earnings regressions and (2) the decision to include in the comparison sample persons without strong labor market ties. When pre-enrollment earnings are controlled for and persons without strong labor market ties are excluded from the comparison sample, Dickinson, Johnson, and West report that Westat's methodology would result in substantially lower net impact estimates of -$529 for adult men and $299 for adult women. This estimate for men is in roughly the same ballpark as the overall estimate of -$690 shown in table 2.2 for the authors' own study. With respect to female CETA participants, it is interesting to note that Dickinson, Johnson, and West conclude that their overall impact estimate reported in the table of just $13 per year is likely to be on the conservative side, and that an estimate on the order of $200 to $300 (i.e., an estimate close to the revised Westat estimate of $299) is more reasonable.

NOTES

1. Also passed in 1962, the Trade Adjustment Assistance (TAA) program was created to provide income support and retraining to workers who lost jobs in industries adversely affected by foreign imports. The TAA program is discussed at greater length in chapter 6 in connection with the Australian Structural Adjustment Assistance (SAA) program.

2. Levitan and Gallo (1988) provide an interesting discussion of the demise of CETA and its replacement by the Job Training Partnership Act (JTPA), along with a spirited defense of CETA.

3. An important exception is Ashenfelter's (1978) study of the impact of MDTA-funded CT programs using as a comparison group a sample drawn from the Continuous Work History Sample maintained by the Social Security Administration. Ashenfelter reports for males that the net impact of training on annual earnings is between $150 and $500 in the year immediately following training, declining to about half these amounts after five years. For females, the net impact estimates are between $300 and $600, with no evidence of a decline in succeeding years.

3
Evidence From U.S.
Demonstration Projects

The CETA program expired in 1982 with the national economy mired in the trough of the deepest recession since the 1930s. Rather than renewing the CETA program with its politically unpopular emphasis on PSE, extended negotiations between President Reagan and Congress resulted in a broad new program—the Job Training Partnership Act (JTPA)—to train and place workers in private-sector jobs. Title III of JTPA is specifically directed at assisting displaced workers.[1] Relative to CETA, the new legislation gives increased responsibility to state governments for planning and implementing displaced worker programs. Moreover, it defines a more active role for the business community in program development through the establishment of Private Industry Councils (PICs). Finally, JTPA differs from CETA in its concentration of resources on training and JSA services rather than PSE and income maintenance and in its requirement that numerical performance standards be used in assessing local program success.

Because many displaced workers failed to satisfy the income test required for program eligibility, the experience gained from CETA programs was of limited usefulness in shaping the direction of new Title III JTPA programs. Rising unemployment and an increasing number of plant closures led the USDOL to begin funding in 1980 a series of demonstration projects intended to test the effectiveness of alternative reemployment services in placing displaced workers in private-sector jobs. This chapter examines the results of four major demonstration projects starting, in chronological order, with the Downriver displaced worker program. Table 3.1 presents an overview of the four demonstrations indicating the time periods during which the programs were in operation, the groups of displaced work-

Table 3.1
Characteristics of Major Displaced Worker Demonstrations

Demonstration project	Time period	Targeted workers	Sample size	Evaluation method
Downriver:				
Phase I	July 1980– Sept. 1981	Experienced male workers laid off from particular auto and auto parts plants	388 treatment; 384 comparison	Comparison group drawn randomly from other auto plants
Phase II	Nov. 1981– Sept. 1983		594 treatment; 341 comparison	
Buffalo:				
Target plant	Oct. 1982– Sept. 1983	Experienced male workers laid off from 6 steel and auto plants	281 treatment; 516 comparison	Random assignment of program slots to treatment and control groups
Nontarget plant		Experienced male workers laid off from 3 other steel and auto plants or from over 300 other establishments	251 treatment; 470 comparison	Self-selected treatment and comparison groups
Texas WAD:				
Houston	1983–85	Mostly male professional workers laid off from petrochemical plants eligible for Title III JTPA programs	470 treatment; 164 control	Random assignment of eligible workers to treatment and control groups
El Paso		Mostly female Hispanic workers laid off from light manufacturing plants eligible for Title III JTPA programs	362 treatment; 312 control	
New Jersey UI project	July 1986– fall 1987	Male and female UI claimants with at least 3 years of tenure	8,675 treatment; 2,385 control	Random assignment of eligible workers to treatment and control groups

ers to which services were targeted, sample sizes, and differences in evaluation methodologies.

The Downriver Program

The Downriver displaced worker program was conceived by the Downriver Community Conference—a consortium representing sixteen communities in the southwestern suburbs of Detroit—in response to the closing of a BASF auto parts plant in April 1980. Downriver staff members moved quickly following the plant closing announcement to develop a service delivery plan to assist in the reemployment of about 700 laid-off BASF workers. During the summer of 1980, the USDOL became interested in the Downriver program as a possible model for the development of a national displaced worker program. An initial federal grant of $1.2 million allowed the program to expand its target population to include 1,100 workers permanently laid off from a nearby DANA auto parts plant. Comparison plants selected for this first phase of the program were a Lear-Siegler Corporation plant and the Chrysler Huber Avenue Foundry, both of which were closed permanently during the summer of 1980. Phase I of the program continued from July 1980 through September 1981.

Based on the first year's performance, an additional federal grant of $3.825 million was awarded to extend Downriver program services to about 2,000 workers laid off from the Ford Motor Company's Michigan Casting Company (MCC) plant. This second phase of the program was in operation from November 1981 to September 1983. Laid off workers from a Chrysler assembly plant and the Chrysler Foundry served as the comparison group in Phase II. Across both phases, program-eligible workers were experienced male production workers above the age of 25 who earned high wages averaging about $10.00 per hour on their pre-displacement jobs. BASF and DANA workers averaged nearly 15 years of tenure on their pre-displacement jobs, while average tenure for Ford MCC workers was about seven years. Most program-eligible workers were married with family responsibilities, and about 31 percent were black. It should be emphasized that workers were not randomly assigned to the treatment and comparison groups. Rather, treatment and comparison group members were randomly selected, respectively, from the treatment and comparison plants.

Recruitment for the Downriver program was plant-based, with the cooperation of employers and the United Auto Workers union in providing rosters of laid-off workers, signing outreach letters, and posting notices in union halls. Substantial rates of program participation of about 48 percent for Phase I and 42 percent for Phase II were achieved. These high participation rates appear to be attributable to the targeting of program services to workers laid off from particular plants, which defined a specific target population of workers and limited the number of employers and local unions that had to be contacted for active involvement in outreach and recruitment efforts.

Eligible displaced workers who opted to participate in the Downriver program were first enrolled in an orientation and testing program, followed by a mandatory four-day job-seeking skills workshop. After completing the workshop, participants who indicated an interest in retraining were evaluated by staff members before referral so that only those likely to benefit were sent on to training programs. Close to 60 percent of participants received some form of retraining with the bulk of these individuals enrolling in classroom training. Only about 13 percent of trainees were enrolled in on-the-job training, in part because OJT positions with local firms were difficult to secure. CT programs were contracted out to local educational institutions, usually under a performance-based contract. Under this contracting scheme, reimbursement of training costs is based partly or entirely on contractor performance as measured by both the number of trainees completing the course and the number of trainees placed in jobs after training.

Table 3.2 indicates the three outcome measures used in the Downriver program evaluation carried out by Abt Associates and reported by Kulik, Smith, and Stromsdorfer (1984). The placement rate measures the percentage of workers ever reemployed during the observation period measured from the date of layoff to the survey interview date. Observation periods for Downriver participants averaged about two-and-one-half years. To capture the stability of

Table 3.2
Net Impact Estimates for Major Displaced Worker Demonstrations[a]

Demon-stration project	Place-ment rate	Employ-ment[c]	Ave. earnings[d]	Ave. wkly. hours	UI benefits[e]	Weeks of UI[f]
Downriver[b]						
Phase I:						
BASF (1)	21.4%**	20.1%**	$110.9**			
(2)	17.0**	18.4**	44.4**			
DANA (1)	18.8*	6.1*	121.8*			
(2)	8.7*	5.8*	33.1*			
Phase II:						
Ford						
MCC (1)	−38.4**	−9.4	−2.3			
(2)	−19.2*	−5.6	−18.9			
Buffalo						
Target plant	31**	33**	115**	13.6%**		
Nontarget plant	6	11	96**	7.6**		
Texas WAD						
Men:						
Houston		2.1wks.	750		−$210	
El Paso		0.7	770		−170	
Women:						
Houston		1.7	0		200	
El Paso		3.1**	1,070**		−130	
New Jersey UI					−108	−0.62

Sources: Downriver: Kulik, Smith, and Stromsdorfer (1984: tables 3.4 and 3.6); Buffalo: Corson, Long, and Maynard (1985: table IV.3); Texas WAD: Bloom and Kulik (1986: exhibit 7.2); and New Jersey: Corson, *et al.* (1989: table 2).

[a]** and * signify that the program effect is statistically significant at the 5 percent and 10 percent confidence levels, respectively.

[b]For Phase I, (1) signifies that Lear-Siegler only is the comparison plant; while (2) signifies that Lear-Siegler and Chrysler Foundry are the comparison plants. For Phase II, (1) signifies that Chrysler Assembly only is the comparison plant; while (2) signifies that Chrysler Assembly and Chrysler Foundry are the comparison plants.

[c]For Downriver and Buffalo, measured as the percentage of weeks employed during the observation period; for Texas WAD, measured as number of weeks worked during post-assignment quarters 3 and 4. Quarterly employment rate estimates for New Jersey are reported in table 3.7.

[d]Measured weekly for Downriver and Buffalo and annually for Texas WAD. Quarterly estimates for New Jersey are reported in table 3.7.

[e]Measured over 30 weeks for Texas WAD and over the benefit year for New Jersey. The New Jersey estimate is constructed as a weighted average of separate treatment effects.

[f]Constructed as a weighted average of separate treatment effects.

employment following layoff, the employment rate measures for each worker the fraction of weeks employed during the observation period. Finally, average weekly earnings are calculated as total earnings from layoff to interview divided by the number of weeks in the observation period. A number of measured variables which differed between the program-eligible and comparison groups and which were thought to influence reemployment experience are controlled for using regression analysis. These control variables include worker characteristics such as age, race, marital status, schooling, work experience, and tenure and occupation in the pre-layoff job. Also included is a dummy variable for each plant. No attempt was made to control for sample selectivity except for the inclusion in the regression models of explanatory variables likely to affect program participation as well as labor market outcomes.

For Phase I of the program, the net impact estimates in table 3.2 indicate that program enrollment increased both the placement rate and the employment rate of former BASF workers by about 20 percentage points. These findings are especially noteworthy because of their robustness across comparison groups. With respect to average weekly earnings, participants enjoyed an increase in earnings over the level they otherwise could have expected of $44 and $111, depending on whether Chrysler Foundry is included in the comparison group. This sensitivity to the composition of the comparison group may reflect, in part, the fact that Chrysler workers were the highest paid and BASF workers the lowest paid prior to layoff of those surveyed. The higher estimate implies an annual earnings gain on the order of $5,545 (assuming a 50-week work year), which is considerably larger than any of the estimates shown in table 2.2 for CETA programs.

Among former DANA workers, the net impact estimates shown in the table for placement rates and especially for employment rates, while still positive, are smaller than those obtained for the BASF group. In addition, the DANA estimates for placement rates are much more sensitive to the composition of the comparison group. On the other hand, the estimated net impact of the program on earnings is roughly the same for former DANA workers as for former

BASF workers with the same degree of sensitivity to the composition of the comparison group.

Turning to Phase II, program participation is seen to have actually reduced the placement rate of former Ford workers during the post-layoff observation period. Participation also has a negative but not statistically significant effect on the employment rate and on weekly earnings. To reconcile this dramatic difference in estimates between the two phases, Kulik, Smith, and Stromsdorfer (1984: 74–82) consider the effects of possible changes in program services and in the characteristics of eligible workers and of the worsening local labor market situation between 1980–81 and 1981–83. They conclude, however, that the most likely explanation lies in the existence of un-measured plant-specific differences that were not completely con-trolled for by the observable variables included in the regression models. Estimated net impacts may thus confound unmeasured plant-specific differences with the true program effects. In particular, im-portant differences in motivation may have existed between DANA and BASF workers and Ford workers. Supporting this conclusion is quantitative evidence indicating a shorter length of program enroll-ment and a lower rate of training completion for Ford workers. An-ecdotal evidence also suggests greater problems of absenteeism and drug abuse in the Ford plant.

The Downriver program also sheds a limited amount of light on the four policy questions posed in chapter 1. Beginning with the is-sue of the effectiveness of alternative program services, the only available comparison for the Downriver program involves CT and JSA. Kulik, Smith, and Stromsdorfer (1984: 82–92) report that av-erage skill training cost per enrollee was more than twice the average cost of JSA and that the program significantly increased access to training programs. Nevertheless, training is found not to have signif-icantly improved participants' reemployment prospects above the as-sistance provided by JSA. The authors qualify this finding with the caveats that (1) the sample sizes are small and (2) workers were not randomly assigned to the CT and JSA-only treatment groups.

Concerning the next two questions, the Downriver program pro-vides evidence regarding program participation in general rather than the receipt of skill training only. Question 2 asks whether some groups benefit more from training than others. The Downriver evaluation results indicate that tenure on the pre-layoff job, age, and a black skin color are negatively related to post-program employment and earnings. Total labor market experience, on the other hand, serves to enhance employment prospects. Question 3 poses the distinction between the effect of training on wage rates as opposed to reemployment. The results shown in table 3.2 for Phase I (but not, as noted, for Phase II) indicate that program participation decreases duration of unemployment and increases weekly earnings, with the impact on earnings for DANA workers being particularly large relative to the impact on unemployment. Without evidence on the effect of the program on weekly hours, however, it is not possible to calculate its impact on average hourly wages.

Worth discussing in some detail is the approach of Downriver program planners to the final question of what to train workers to do. Downriver staff members first attempted to identify occupations for which demand was expected to grow in the local labor market. This task was accomplished by reviewing economic forecasts and studies conducted by local universities, studying trade journals, and analyzing labor market data collected by the Michigan Employment Security (ES) commission. Next, the actual demand for labor in the occupations that survived this scrutiny was verified through interviews with local employers and representatives of trade associations. Kulik, Smith, and Stromsdorfer (1984: 30) emphasize, however, that

> [P]rogram staff were *not* interested in identifying *firm-specific* labor needs for which "customized" training would need to be developed, as staff considered this a risky investment. Rather, they preferred to train for occupations for which there was sufficient demand on the part of a number of employers, so that participants' reemployment prospects were not tied to the fortunes of only one firm.

Once the decision on occupations was arrived upon, Downriver officials invited local educational institutions to participate in designing curricula suitable for class-size training programs.

The Dislocated Worker Demonstration Project

Responding to widespread layoffs and plant closings during the early 1980s, the USDOL launched the Dislocated Worker Demonstration Project in October 1982 with the objective of gaining a better understanding of how best to reduce the adjustment costs borne by workers displaced from jobs in major manufacturing industries. While the Downriver program provided some guidance for developing new displaced worker program, USDOL officials took the position that it was important to test additional program models in different economic environments. In addition, the Downriver net impact estimates are difficult to interpret because of the striking differences between the two phases of the project and the sensitivity of even Phase I impact estimates to the choice of comparison plants. To provide firmer evidence on the effectiveness of retraining and other services in assisting displaced workers, demonstration grants were awarded to six sponsoring organizations scattered throughout the country. The sponsoring organizations were located in Alameda County, California; Buffalo; Milwaukee; Lehigh Valley, Pennsylvania; Mid-Willamette Valley, Oregon; and Yakima County, Washington. Concurrently, a seventh project funded by state, local, and private-sector sources was implemented in the Southgate area of Los Angeles. The six projects plus the Southgate program served over 10,000 displaced workers between October 1, 1982 and September 30, 1983.

The Buffalo Dislocated Worker Program

Early in the evaluation design process, it was decided that due to cost considerations the impact analysis should be limited to one site only. The Buffalo program was chosen as the impact analysis site, primarily because it offered a true control group for the majority of the workers recruited for participation in the program.[2] It was also a relatively successful program among the six sites, as measured by short-term performance indicators such as the overall placement rate. Referring back to table 3.1, the Buffalo program is seen to be quite similar to Downriver in terms of the target population of displaced workers. In fact, Corson, Long, and Maynard (1985: 11) note that the Buffalo impact evaluation has the advantage that in some respects it can be viewed as a replication of the Downriver evaluation. On the other hand, the ability to generalize from the evaluation findings is limited by the decision to carry out the net impact analysis only for Buffalo.

Buffalo program services were offered to two groups of displaced workers—(1) mostly steel and auto workers displaced during 1982 from nine area plants, and (2) a more heterogeneous group of workers permanently laid off after 1980 from over 300 area establishments. About 30 percent of program slots were reserved for the latter group. The program used three different procedures for selecting workers for program participation. First, available program slots were rationed through a formal lottery mechanism among workers from six of the nine target plants. Thus, displaced workers in what is termed the "target-plant sample" who were offered program services (or recruited) are a random sample of all workers from these six plants. Nonrecruited workers from these plants would represent a natural control group. Second, all workers from the three remaining target plants were recruited for the program. Finally, workers from the over-300 area establishments were offered program services on a first-come, first-served basis as program slots become available. Recruited workers from the three remaining target plants and from the over-300 area establishments are termed the "nontarget-plant sample." For each of the two samples, labor market outcomes observed for program participants are compared to those observed for a comparison group consisting of (1) recruited individuals who chose not to participate when offered services, and (2) individuals who were not offered services.

Most of the personal and job-related characteristics of recruited workers in the target-plant and nontarget-plant samples are quite similar, with recruited workers being predominantly married white males between the ages of 25 and 55 working full time in blue-collar jobs prior to their displacement. In addition, recruited workers in both groups experienced lengthy periods of post-displacement unemployment prior to program participation. On average, target-plant workers had been laid off more than a year before the start of the program, while those in the nontarget-plant sample had been laid off for about eight weeks. The other major difference between the two samples is that the pre-layoff hourly wage of recruited workers in the target-plant sample averaged $10.78, as opposed to an average pre-layoff wage of $8.70 for recruited nontarget-plant workers. Length of pre-layoff tenure was 10.1 years and 8.5 years, respectively, for recruited target-plant and nontarget-plant workers.

Buffalo Program Evaluation Results

It was noted earlier in this chapter that the Downriver program achieved participation rates among recruited workers approaching 50 percent. Complicating the evaluation of the Buffalo program carried out by Mathematica Policy Research are the much lower participation rates for workers offered program services in both samples (16 percent among recruited target-plant workers and 28 percent among nontarget-plant workers who applied and were offered services). These low participation rates raise the possibility of selection bias due to nonrandom assignment or selection of displaced workers into the treatment and comparison groups. For the target-plant sample, selection bias arises because recruited workers who chose not to participate in the program are included along with nonrecruited workers from the same target plants in the comparison group. In addition to this problem, the comparison group available for the nontarget-plant sample is further contaminated by the presence of eligible workers from the over-300 area enterprises who (1) chose not to apply for program services, or (2) applied for services but were not chosen by program staff members.

As described in the evaluation report by Corson, Long, and Maynard (1985: 100–104), the selection bias problem is dealt with by first explicitly modeling program participation. The parameter estimates of the participation equation are then used to construct a selectivity variable (i.e., the inverse Mill's ratio) which is included as a regressor in each post-program outcome equation. The program estimates shown in table 3.2 are calculated using this econometric approach to (hopefully) obtain program effects free of selection bias.

All four outcome variables displayed in the table are measured for the first six post-program months.

Beginning with target-plant workers, the results in table 3.2 indicate that program participation has a statistically significant effect on placement and employment rates as well as on weekly hours and earnings. These effects are quite large, exceeding in size the Downriver Phase I results for the same outcome variables. Expressing the coefficient estimates as percentages of pre-program mean values, participation in the Buffalo project more than doubled the proportion of time spent employed and increased the placement rate by more than one-half. Increases in average weekly hours and average weekly earnings are 135 percent and 195 percent, respectively, suggesting that the program may have boosted hourly wages for those reemployed, at least in the short run. For the nontarget-plant sample, the point estimates obtained are uniformly smaller than for the target-plant sample; and the main program impacts appear to be increases in weekly hours and average earnings as opposed to improvements in employment opportunities.

Corson, Long, and Maynard (1985: 110–17) also report impact estimates broken down by program treatment and demographic subgroups. With respect to program treatments, the Buffalo site, as was the case for all six sites in the demonstration project, offered participants a full range of services including JSA, CT, and OJT. Following initial orientation and assessment sessions, all Buffalo participants were required to attend a four-day job search workshop. About 45 percent of program participants were then channeled into either CT or OJT positions. Area employers at each of the six sites were offered a 50 percent wage subsidy to develop OJT slots, and the Buffalo program provided the highest proportion of OJT positions among the six sites. The 55 percent of participants who did not receive CT or OJT were assigned to counselors/resource coordinators and offered job development and referral services. The Buffalo program also maintained a resource center to be used by workers in conducting their own job search.

For the employment rate and average weekly earnings, table 3.3 presents net impact estimates disaggregated by program treatment.

Table 3.3
Estimated Program Impacts for the Buffalo Dislocated Worker
Project, by Principal Program Treatment

Outcome variable and principal program treatment	Target-plant sample	Nontarget-plant sample
Employment rate:		
CT	47**	46**
OJT	18	13
JSA-only	33**	-6
Average weekly earnings:		
CT	$122	$141
OJT	64	136**
JSA-only	134**	15

Source: Corson, Long and Maynard (1985: table IV.4).
Note: ** signifies that the program effect is statistically significant at the 5 percent confidence level.

Among target-plant workers, the results indicate that JSA and CT had large effects of roughly the same magnitude on both outcome measures. The strong results for CT, but not for JSA, also carried over to the nontarget-plant estimates. Drawing on the more reliable results for the target-plant sample, Corson, Long, and Maynard (1985: 111–13) point out that JSA is the more cost effective of the two treatments. The reason is that the additional effects (if any) of CT above those of JSA are not large enough to compensate for the higher cost of CT services. (Average costs per participants were $851 for JSA-only, $3,282 for CT with JSA, and $3,170 for OJT with JSA.) Note that the absence of an incremental effect of CT echos the similar finding obtained for the earlier Downriver program. Corson, Long, and Maynard caution, however, that many CT participants completed their training near the end of the demonstration period and thus received relatively little placement assistance. Interestingly, OJT is seen not to have much of an impact on either the employment rate or average earnings for the target-plant sample; but it is statistically significant in increasing average earnings for nontarget-plant workers. Since OJT was primarily used in the Buffalo program as a placement tool, the absence of an effect on employment opportunities suggests that the OJT treatment was unnecessary.

Net program effects are also available broken down by sex, race, age, education, wages and tenure on the pre-displacement job, and availability of income support from Supplemental Unemployment Benefit (SUB) programs. Focusing on proportion of time employed for the target-plant sample, program impacts are found to be greater for women than men, for individuals under age 45 than for those older, and for workers with more than 10 years of tenure on their pre-layoff job than for those with less tenure. Time spent employed did not appear to be strongly affected by race, education, pre-layoff wages, and availability of SUB income support. The result for SUB support is important because it suggests, at least for Buffalo project participants, that the availability of income-maintenance support did not affect their response to program services.

Beyond the net impact results appearing in tables 3.2 and 3.3, Corson, Long, and Maynard (1985) present a comparison of the characteristics of the reemployment job with those of the pre-layoff job. This analysis shows that, on average, weekly hours were reduced from 5 to 10 percent, but that an even larger reduction occurred in weekly earnings, particularly for the relatively high wage target-plant sample. For the target-plant group, about one-third had weekly earnings of less than 50 percent of their pre-layoff weekly earnings, while less than 20 percent showed an increase. Considerable occupational shifting also occurred, reflecting a substantial movement of workers to new jobs outside manufacturing, which had been the industrial sector in which a majority of the pre-layoff jobs were located.

One final note on the Buffalo project relates to the design of CT programs. Corson, Maynard, and Wichita (1984: 75–77) point out in their overview report on all six demonstration sites that the one-year duration of the project severely limited both the careful selection of high growth occupations and the necessary testing and assessment required to insure that participants possessed the motivation and necessary academic skills to benefit from formal classroom training. In general, CT was limited to those occupations and training deliverers amenable to short-duration, high-intensity courses developed on short notice. Local employer involvement in the design of training programs typically took the form of recommendations of PIC committees based on ". . . a relatively unsystematic impression of labor-market demand" (Corson, Maynard, and Wichita 1984: 76).

The Texas Worker Adjustment
Demonstration Projects

JTPA Title III funds began to flow to employment and training assistance programs for displaced workers in October 1982. To understand more completely the labor market effects of these programs, the Texas Department of Community Affairs designed and implemented the experimental Worker Adjustment Demonstration (WAD) projects operated at six sites between 1983 and 1985. Available for evaluation purposes are two projects in El Paso and one in Houston. In comparison to the Downriver and Buffalo projects, an important distinguishing feature of the WAD projects is that they represent an attempt to evaluate an ongoing displaced worker program. In addition, as noted in table 3.1, WAD program services were provided to groups of displaced workers other than the mostly white male steel and auto workers who were targeted for assistance in the Downriver and Buffalo projects. Perhaps most important, the WAD projects applied a true experimental methodology including random assignment of eligible workers.

As described in the Abt Associates report by Bloom and Kulik (1986), the experimental design of the WAD projects allowed Title III program participants to be assigned randomly to either of two treatment groups or to a control group. The treatment groups were supplied services by Texas' established Title III service delivery system. The first treatment group (called Tier I) received JSA services only. Core JSA services provided at all three sites included orientation, job search workshops, assessment, and job development and placement. Members of the second treatment group received JSA followed, if necessary, by more expensive classroom or on-the-job retraining (the Tier I/II sequence). The control group was not eligible for WAD services, but its members were informed of other non-Title III services available in their communities. One difference in the experimental design between the Buffalo program and the WAD projects should be emphasized. In the Buffalo target-plant sample, program slots were allocated randomly among eligible workers, but recruited workers made their own decision on whether to participate in the program and recruited nonparticipants are included in the comparison group. In the WAD projects, in contrast, eligible workers were rationed randomly to the treatment and control groups so that recruited nonparticipants are not included in the control group.

It might also be noted that the low rate of participation for workers offered program services that plagued the Buffalo program was not a problem for the WAD projects, with 71 percent of those assigned to the WAD treatment groups choosing to participate. Bloom and Kulik (1986: 29–31) mention, in particular, that shortfalls between the number of planned and actual participants occurred almost exclusively in connection with Tier II services; and these shortfalls were mainly the result of overestimating provider capacity rather than exaggerating workers' interest. In Houston, in addition, there was an important mismatch between the types of Tier II services supplied and the demand of the client population. This mismatch will be discussed at greater length later in this section.

Beyond the Tier I and Tier I/II distinction, there were also important differences between the WAD sites in Houston and El Paso. In terms of workers' personal and job-related characteristics, over 80 percent of those recruited and assigned to treatment and control groups in the Houston project were male and about 57 percent were white. Also represented in Houston were sizable groups of blacks and Asians. In the two El Paso sites, in contrast, approximately 90 percent of program eligibles were Hispanic and a majority were women. These differences by race and sex primarily reflect the industrial orientation of the projects, with the Houston program targeting its services to highly educated, largely white-collar professional workers laid off from petrochemical plants. In contrast, both El Paso programs focused on workers with much less education displaced from apparel, food processing, and other light manufacturing jobs. Mirroring this difference in industry orientation, the average hourly wage of Houston's eligibles was slightly over $13.00, as compared to about $5.00 for eligible workers in El Paso. Rather surprisingly, most WAD eligibles in all three sites had been employed in their pre-layoff jobs for less than five years—a considerably shorter period of time than the seven to fifteen years of pre-layoff tenure reported for Downriver and Buffalo displaced workers. It is perhaps worth noting that, since the benchmark analysis of displaced workers by Flaim and Sehgal (1985), three years of job tenure has commonly been used to distinguish the displaced from other unemployed workers.

One final difference between WAD sites is that only for the Houston site could the differential effect of the additional services in the Tier I/II sequence be distinguished from Tier I JSA-only services. The program outcome measures available for the El Paso sites are limited to a comparison of the Tier I/II sequence and the control group.

The WAD demonstration yielded three main results. As summarized in table 3.2, the first is that program participants experienced short-run positive impacts on annual earnings and weeks worked, as well as a decrease in dollars received in UI benefits. (The ambiguous findings for female participants in the Houston site appear to be due to a small sample size.) More important, these impact estimates tend to be larger and more pronounced for women than for men. In particular, female participants in El Paso experienced a program-induced gain in annual earnings of $1,070. The gains in annual earnings for men in Houston and El Paso were only $750 and $770, respectively. Since the mostly white male Houston participants earned more than twice as much as the mostly Hispanic female El Paso participants prior to WAD enrollment, the gender difference in estimated earnings gains is even more striking when expressed percentage terms.

A second result emerges from quarter-by-quarter program impact estimates calculated by sex across all three sites and shown in table 3.4. A large and statistically significant earnings gain of $500 occurred for men in the second post-assignment quarter only, and the total net impact estimate for the year is not significantly different from zero due to its large standard error. The time pattern in these results indicates that the main effect of the program was to enable male participants to find jobs sooner than would have otherwise been the case. But ultimately, the employment opportunities of pro-

Table 3.4
Estimated Program Impact on Quarterly
Earnings for the Texas WAD Projects, by Sex

Earnings in post-assignment quarter	Men	Women
Quarter 1	$110	$480**
Quarter 2	500**	330**
Quarter 3	40	160
Quarter 4	130	−110
Total	790	890**

Source: Bloom and Kulik (1986: exhibit 7.1).
Note: ** signifies that the program is statistically significant at the 5 percent level.

gram participants were no better and the wages of participants no higher than for members of the control group. For women, similarly, WAD participation increased earnings on average by $480 in the first post-program quarter, followed by gradually decaying impacts for subsequent quarters. For the year as a whole, however, Bloom and Kulik report a statistically significant net impact estimate of $890, suggesting that female participants may have enjoyed a permanent gain from program participation.[3]

The final result involves the differential effect of Tier I versus Tier I/II services for males in the Houston program. Average program costs per participant were $1,531 for Tier I and $4,991 for Tier I/II. Consistent with the results of the Downriver and Buffalo projects, skill training (which was almost exclusively classroom training) fails to increase earnings and employment above the effects of JSA-only services. In fact, taking at face value the net impact estimates shown in table 3.5, the differential impact of retraining is seen to be *negative* for annual earnings and weeks worked. The incremental effect of retraining services on total UI benefits is exactly zero.

Bloom and Kulik (1986: 170–73) take considerable care in interpreting these negative results for skill training. One explanation they offer is that the addition of a retraining program is likely to cause participants to delay undertaking serious job search until after the training period is completed. If, as just indicated, the primary program effect for men is to expedite their reemployment and this effect

Table 3.5
**Net Impact Estimates for Men in the Houston WAD Project,
by Program Treatment**

Outcome measure	Tier I-only	TierI/II	Differential impact
Earnings for the post-assignment year	$860	$680	−$180
Weeks worked in post-assignment quarters 3 and 4	4.3**	0.6	−3.7
Total UI benefits for the 30 week post-assignment period	−$220	−$220	0

Source: Bloom and Kulik (1986: exhibit 7.3).
Note: ** signifies that the program effect is statistically significant at the 5 percent level.

occurs soon after the receipt of JSA services, a delay in beginning the job search process will reduce reemployment rates.

A second explanation considered more realistic by the authors is the mismatch between the retraining opportunities offered and the interests and backgrounds of the target group. The classroom training programs provided by the Houston Community College were primarily technical/vocational in nature, offering retraining in occupations including air conditioning and refrigeration and computer maintenance technology. At the same time, as noted, Houston program participants were well educated, highly paid former white-collar workers who presumably had little interest in training courses in skilled manual trades. Further complicating matters was a lack of integration of the JSA and CT program components caused by poor communication between the Tier I and Tier II contractors. It is therefore not surprising that the take-up of retraining was low and the payoff limited. In their recommendations for future Title III programming, Bloom and Kulik (1986: 179–82) suggest that (1) JSA should be the core service provided in displaced worker programs, and (2) skill training should be offered to fewer, more carefully screened participants who can be better matched to training opportunities that are potentially available in the community. At the same time, however, they conclude that the cost effectiveness of high quality, accurately targeted skill training remains an open issue.

The New Jersey UI Reemployment
Demonstration Project

Like the Texas WAD projects, the New Jersey Unemployment Insurance (UI) Reemployment Demonstration was intended to examine the effectiveness of an ongoing program—in this case, the operation of the UI system. The UI system provides short-term income support to involuntarily unemployed individuals while they actively seek work. It also attempts to assist in the reemployment of unemployed workers by referring them either to the ES for placement services or to retraining programs offered under JTPA. In recent years, however, a number of critics of the present UI system have argued that the primary reemployment problem encountered by workers displaced from their jobs by plant closures or mass layoffs is not one of riding out a temporary spell of unemployment until a cyclical upturn occurs. Since the displaced face longer-term reemployment difficulties, these critics suggest instead that what is needed is the targeting of more intensive reemployment assistance, including skill training, to permanently separated UI claimants who would otherwise be unable to qualify for vacant jobs in growing industries.[4] To increase their effectiveness, moreover, both critics and supporters of the present UI system agree that these reemployment services should be provided before or soon after layoffs take place (see Leigh 1989: chap. 4).

Initiated by the USDOL and operated as a joint venture by the USDOL and the New Jersey Department of Labor, the New Jersey Demonstration was implemented in July 1986 and program services were continued into the fall of 1987. In response to the recent criticisms of the UI system, the project had two primary objectives. The first is to assess the feasibility of an "early intervention" strategy. At issue are the questions of whether and how it is possible to use the UI system to identify early in the claim period unemployed workers who are likely to face prolonged spells of unemployment and exhaust UI benefits. "Early" is defined operationally as the fifth week of claiming UI benefits.

The Demonstration's second objective is to empirically measure the effectiveness of three alternative packages of reemployment services in accelerating the return to work. The three packages of services—designated Treatments 1, 2, and 3, respectively—are JSA-only, JSA combined with training or relocation assistance, and JSA combined with a cash bonus for early reemployment. Demonstration services were provided at each of 10 sites by four-person teams consisting of three ES staff members and a JTPA staff member from the local Service Delivery Area operator. ES staff provided all of the services for the JSA-only and JSA plus reemployment bonus treatments, and existing JTPA local program operators were responsible for identifying appropriate training opportunities and placing claimants in training programs.

Program Design and Implementation

Beginning with the first objective, the basic problem is to distinguish displaced workers from those unemployed for cyclical, frictional, or seasonal reasons, so that "unneeded" services are not provided to workers reasonably anticipating recall to their old jobs or otherwise expected to have little difficulty in locating new employment. The clearest way to make this distinction is by looking at the length of completed unemployment spells. The longer the spell, the more likely it is that an unemployed worker is truly displaced. Unfortunately, this approach is not of much help in making decisions early in the spell of unemployment on which workers should be targeted for assistance. Assistance might also be restricted to workers displaced from their jobs by a mass permanent layoff or a plant closure. This was the targeting strategy used in the Downriver project described earlier. But this approach neglects the adjustment assistance needs of job losers adversely affected by the ripple effect of a large plant closure or mass layoff in causing suppliers to the closed plant and local retail and service outlets to lay off employees.

The approach taken by New Jersey program designers to distinguish the displaced from other unemployed workers was to apply five "screens" during the fourth week of claiming benefits. The cumulative effect of these screens is to define the displaced to be UI claimants 25 years of age and older who had at least three years of tenure with their last employer prior to being laid off and who could not provide a specific date at which they expected to be recalled. As noted in table 3.1, slightly more than 11,000 claimants passed through these screens during the July 1986–June 1987 period and were randomly assigned to the three treatment groups and the control group. Men and women were about equally represented in the eligible population, and there were sizable proportions of blacks (17.2 percent) and Hispanics (19.5 percent) as well as of workers age 55 and older (22 percent). Regarding industry mix, about 47 percent of the eligible population was laid off from manufacturing jobs; 20 percent and 16 percent, respectively, were displaced from jobs in wholesale and retail trade and services. The average pre-layoff wage for eligible workers was $403 per week, and about two-thirds of these workers were employed five years or longer on their pre-layoff jobs.

Turning to the second objective of the Demonstration, all three treatments began with a common set of initial services delivered, starting in the fifth week of unemployment. After receipt of a notification letter, claimants were to report to a Demonstration office (usually an ES office) for orientation and testing. In the following week, they attended a week-long, half-day job search workshop. This was followed a week later by a one-on-one counseling/assessment session. These initial services were considered mandatory, and failure to report could lead to the denial of UI benefits.

Beginning with the counseling/assessment interview, the services offered to members of the three treatment groups diverged. Claimants receiving Treatment 1 services—the JSA-only group—were expected to make periodic contact with the Demonstration office, either by stopping by to discuss job search activities with staff members or by making use of the resource center situated in the office. Resource centers typically contained job listings, telephones, and occupational and training literature.

Claimants in the second treatment group were also informed about the resource center and the requirement to maintain periodic contact with the Demonstration office during the job search process. In addition, they were offered the opportunity to enroll in a CT or OJT program. Acceptable CT programs—which were offered by a wide range of public and private training providers—were subject to the restrictions that their expected duration not exceed six months and that remedial education be offered only if necessary to enable claimants to progress to vocational training courses. The two major areas of CT were business and office and computer and information sciences. Corson *et al.* (1989: 109, 111) note that the average cost per trainee of CT ($2,723) was low in comparison to the typical experience in New Jersey JTPA programs because the courses were designed to upgrade claimants' skills rather than to provide training in a whole new vocational area. An example they cite of skill upgrading is that an individual with accounting skills might be trained to use a spreadsheet package on a personal computer.

Employers who provided OJT slots to claimants eligible for Treatment 2 services received a wage subsidy of 50 percent; and about half of the OJT jobs were in technical, clerical, and sales occupations. Average cost of OJT per trainee was $1,960. Finally, Treatment 2 claimants were told about the availability of relocation assistance which, if they elected not to pursue training, could be used to pay for moving expenses and for job interview trips exceeding 50 miles in length. Consistent with the experience of earlier demonstrations, very few Treatment 2 claimants opted to take advantage of relocation assistance.

The reemployment bonus concept made operational in Treatment 3 is directed at the problem that the reemployment of displaced workers may be delayed, not by inadequate job search skills, but by a lack of motivation to engage in search or by the natural reluctance to accept a new job offering considerably lower wages and benefits than the pre-layoff job.[5] The New Jersey reemployment bonus treatment worked as follows. During the counseling/assessment interview, claimants selected for this treatment were informed of the specifics of the bonus program. If they decided to participate, they could collect the maximum bonus by locating and accepting a job during the next two weeks. The maximum bonus was specified to be one-half of the claimant's remaining UI entitlement at the time of the interview. (The maximum bonus averaged $1,644.) After the two-week period had passed, the size of the bonus decreased by 10 percent per week, reaching zero at the end of the eleventh week after the counseling/ assessment interview. A bonus payment was made only to participants who obtained full-time employment with a new employer lasting four weeks or longer. Furthermore, the payment of the bonus was tied to length of job tenure. At the end of four weeks of employment, the claimant received 60 percent of the bonus with the remaining 40 percent received only after 12 weeks of employment.

With the exception of the reemployment bonus and relocation assistance, the Demonstration services were similar to existing JTPA retraining programs and ES placement assistance supplied to unemployed New Jersey residents. An important difference is that claimants in the Demonstration had a considerably higher chance of receiving services. Moreover, Demonstration services were generally provided earlier in the unemployment spell than were existing services.

Evaluation Results

The evaluation of the New Jersey Demonstration was carried out by Mathematica Policy Research. Corson and Kerachsky (1987) discuss preliminary results for the first six months of program operation following its implementation in July 1986, and Corson et al. (1989) present final program evaluation results. Regarding the Demonstration's first objective, Corson et al. suggest that the five screens used do satisfactorily identify claimants who, in the absence of additional employment services, would be likely to experience difficulty in becoming reemployed. Sizable fractions of the eligible population were older, previously employed in manufacturing, and displaced from their jobs by a plant closure or the elimination of a shift. Moreover, the eligible population includes a substantial proportion of black and Hispanic workers. It is also important to note that the eligible population experienced longer UI durations and a higher UI exhaustion rate than the ineligible population. Cases in which the screening procedure tended to break down include individuals from growing industries like services, and claimants who eventually returned to their former employer and presumably did not require program services.

With respect to the second objective, strengths of the New Jersey Demonstration are its broad coverage of state residents and its large sample size. As is true for the Buffalo demonstration project, however, the assessment of Treatment 2 services is made more difficult by a low degree of participation in retraining programs. Of those who passed through the counseling/assessment interview and were offered training, only about 15 percent chose to participate. Most of these participants were enrolled in a CT program. While this participation rate is higher than the rate for noneligible claimants exposed to regular JTPA retraining services, it is not as high as might be expected on the basis of earlier demonstration projects. Corson *et al.* (1989: 113–15) speculate that this lower than expected participation rate may be because (1) the offer of retraining early in the layoff period comes before claimants recognize that they could benefit from training services; (2) program eligible claimants who agreed to assessment and counseling sessions (and were offered training) as a requirement to collect UI would presumably be less interested in training programs than those who attended the initial sessions voluntarily, as was the case for some other demonstrations; and (3) inadequacies in the screening procedure mean that some individuals offered training simply did not need it.

Since Treatments 1 and 3, in particular, are intended to lead to more rapid reemployment of participating claimants, it is expected that the amount of UI benefits received by treatment group members will be less than the amount received by the control group. This expectation is borne out in the negative and statistically significant net impact estimates in table 3.6. Although random assignment assures in principle that differences in mean outcomes for the treatment groups and the control group provide unbiased net impact estimates, the estimates reported are coefficients estimated from a simple regression model containing dummy variables to represent the three treatments and controlling for differences in claimants' individual characteristics, ES offices, and the timing of sample selection.

Looking first at the JSA-only treatment in table 3.6, program participation reduces UI benefits by $87 over the benefit year—an estimate that is considerably less than the -$200 calculated over 30

Table 3.6

**Estimated Program Impacts on UI Receipt for the New Jersey
UI Reemployment Demonstration, by Program Treatment**

UI measure	JSA-only	JSA plus training	JSA plus reemployment bonus
Dollars paid in benefit year	−87*	−81*	−170***
Weeks paid in benefit year	−0.47*	−0.48**	−0.97***
Weeks paid in first spell	−0.59**	−0.53**	−0.93**
Exhaustion rate	−0.028**	−0.017	−0.037***

Source: Corson et al. (1989: table 2).
Note: *, **, and *** signify that the program effect is statistically significant at the 10, 5, and 1 percent confidence levels, respectively.

weeks for the Texas WAD projects. The $87 estimate represents about a 3 percent reduction in average benefits paid to the control group. JSA-only is further seen to decrease weeks of UI receipt during the first UI spell and during the benefit year and to reduce the exhaustion rate of claimants. The slightly larger effect for weeks paid in the first spell than for weeks paid over the entire benefit year suggests that a few individuals who stopped collecting UI because of JSA subsequently collected additional benefits later in their benefit year.

Skipping over Treatment 2 for the moment, JSA plus the reemployment bonus is expected to have the largest impact of the three treatments because of the substantial reemployment incentive created by the bonus. The differences between Treatment 3 and Treatment 1 estimates are significantly different from zero indicating a sizable incremental effect of the bonus in speeding up reemployment. Corson et al. (1989: 266) suggest that the more appropriate comparison is between Treatment 1 and 3 claimants who received the counseling/ assessment interview. Focusing on these individuals, the reemployment bonus offer by itself reduced UI benefits by $101 over the benefit year and weeks paid in the benefit year by 0.69. These estimates are somewhat smaller than the impacts of UI receipt—reductions of $158 in benefit payments and 1.15 weeks paid over the benefit year—estimated by Woodbury and Spiegelman (1987) for the Illinois Claimant Bonus Experiment.[6]

Treatment 2 is expected to have the smallest short-run effect on UI receipt of the three treatments since individuals undergoing training continued to receive UI benefits. Consistent with this expectation, the impact estimates presented in table 3.6 indicate that the offer of training assistance on top of the basic JSA services provided in Treatment 1 did not appreciably affect the UI outcomes examined. This result is understandable since the low take-up rate of the offer of training would dilute any program effect when measured over the entire treatment group.

Table 3.7 expands the net impact analysis to include estimates of the effects of the three program treatments on proportion of time employed, earnings, and the post-UI wage rate. Data on the first two of these outcome measures are obtained from a follow-up interview that allows the measurement of quarter-by-quarter effects for the first four quarters following the claim filing date. State administrative records, which do not lend themselves to measuring the timing of program impacts, are the source of the wage data. For Treatment 1, the first quarter impact of JSA is to raise the employment rate of program participants 2.3 percentage points above that of the control group. As indicated in the table, this estimate represents a 16.2 percent increase in employment relative to the control group mean. In subsequent quarters, the point estimates are higher, but they represent smaller percentages of control group means, and the percentage impact estimates decline over time. Similarly, the quarterly earnings estimates show a large initial impact of 18.2 percent, which declines over time to essentially zero by quarter 4. Taken in conjunction with the quarterly earnings estimates displayed in table 3.4 for the Texas WAD projects, this evidence appears to be quite clear in indicating that JSA is effective in encouraging rapid reemployment. Its relatively low cost, moreover, means that in the cost-benefit analysis performed by Corson et al.

JSA comes the closest of the three treatments to paying for itself in terms of reduced UI outlays.

Turning to Treatment 2, the quarterly net impact estimates shown in table 3.7 for JSA plus training are uniformly smaller than those for JSA only (with the exception of earnings in quarter 4). This result is not unexpected since individuals enrolled in training would remain unemployed for the duration of their training program. Rather than a significant short-run effect, the benefits of retraining are expected to show up in the longer run as upgraded skills pay off in increased employment stability and possibly higher wages. In an attempt to measure the longer-run impact of training, earnings impacts in quarters 5 and 6 were estimated with the result that Treatment 2 had no discernable effect in either quarter. (The point estimates are $2 in quarter 5 and -$124 in quarter 6, and neither estimate is statistically significant.) Before interpreting these results as further evidence of the ineffectiveness of skill training, however, Corson *et al.* (1989: 14) caution that

> . . . since relatively few individuals in the JSA plus training treatment actually received training, and since sufficient time had not elapsed to observe post-training employment outcomes for all these individuals, these findings should be considered inconclusive as they pertain to the value of training per se for the demonstration-eligible population.

The Treatment 3 results presented in table 3.7 indicate for the first two quarters that JSA plus the offer of a reemployment bonus has a larger impact on employment and earnings than JSA-only. These differences between treatment impacts, however, are not as large as might be expected on the basis of the results in table 3.6 for UI receipt. By quarter 3, the effects of Treatment 3 on employment and earnings are seen to have declined sharply; and the quarter 3 and quarter 4 estimates are exceeded by the corresponding JSA-only estimates. It seems reasonable to conclude that the impact of Treatment 3 on employment and earnings primarily represents the early reemployment generated by JSA.

An important concern, especially with respect to the reemployment bonus, is that the effect of the treatments in accelerating reem-

Table 3.7
Estimated Program Impacts on Employment, Earnings, and Post-UI Wages for the New Jersey UI Reemployment Demonstration, by Program Treatment

Outcome measure	JSA-only	JSA plus training	JSA plus reemployment bonus
Employment rate:			
Quarter 1	2.3**	1.9**	2.8***
	(16.2)	(13.4)	(19.7)
Quarter 2	4.2***	2.8*	5.0***
	(12.4)	(7.0)	(12.6)
Quarter 3	4.3**	2.2	2.3
	(7.7)	(3.9)	(4.1)
Quarter 4	2.8	1.7	0.6
	(4.5)	(2.7)	(1.0)
Earnings:			
Quarter 1	$125**	$82	$160***
	(18.2)	(11.9)	(23.3)
Quarter 2	263**	103	278***
	(13.5)	(5.3)	(14.3)
Quarter 3	171	83	131
	(6.3)	(3.1)	(4.9)
Quarter 4	49	77	22
	(1.6)	(2.6)	(0.7)
% change in post-UI wage relative to pre-UI wage	0.041**	0.030**	0.041**

Source: Corson *et al.* (1989: tables VI.2–VI.7 and VI.11).

Notes: Quarters are defined relative to the date of the initial UI claim, and numbers in parentheses are impact estimates expressed as percentages of control group means. *, **, and *** signify that the program effect is statistically significant at the 10, 5, and 1 percent levels, respectively.

ployment may have occurred because participants accepted a less favorable job match (thereby sacrificing earnings). The hourly wage results shown in the last row of table 3.7 suggest that this concern is groundless. In fact, all three treatments appear to have led to a modest increase in the wages paid in post-UI jobs. Woodbury and Spiegelman (1987) report a similar finding for the Illinois Claimant Bonus Experiment. Their conclusion is that the faster reemployment of Illinois program participants resulted from more intense job search effort, and not from overly rapid acceptance of job offers.

In addition to the results described in tables 3.6 and 3.7, Corson *et al.* provide an analysis of the impact of the treatments disaggregated by population subgroups. This analysis suggests that the treatments were most successful at promoting the reemployment of displaced workers possessing marketable skills, such as clerical and other white-collar workers. The treatments were less successful in assisting those workers the authors describe as facing "hard-core, structural unemployment problems." The latter group includes blue-collar workers, workers displaced from jobs in durable-goods manufacturing, and permanently separated workers. One reason for the relatively favorable reemployment prospects of white-collar workers is found in recent evidence indicating that there is a high degree of transferability of skills for this group. Using 1984 DWS data for men, Kletzer (1989) shows that there is an important difference between blue-collar workers and managerial, professional, and technical workers in the contribution of pre-displacement job tenure to explaining post-displacement weekly earnings. To bring out this point, she calculates the following earnings elasticities with respect to tenure on the old and new jobs:

	Blue-collar	White-collar
Old job	.02673	.03224
New job	.00691	.02613

These estimates suggest that the marginal contribution of previous job tenure to post-displacement earnings is just 25.8 percent of its contribution to pre-displacement earnings for blue-collar workers (.258 = .00691/.02673). For white-collar workers, on the other hand, this percentage rises to 81.0 percent. In other words, the skills possessed by blue-collar workers are more likely to be job-specific and thus nontransferable to the post-displacement job than those possessed by white-collar workers.

The conclusion that New Jersey Demonstration services were primarily of assistance to displaced workers who already enjoyed relatively favorable reemployment prospects is not terribly surprising in view of the fact, noted earlier, that CT was designed to upgrade existing skills rather than to develop entirely new skills. Despite the absence of a measurable short-run effect of skill training, Corson *et al.* (1989: 342) therefore argue that longer-run, more intensive services are needed for displaced workers who face major structural dislocations. In support of this argument, they cite the high rate at which otherwise eligible workers were excused from testing and job search workshops as evidence suggesting that referrals to English-as-a-Second-Language or remedial education services may be needed for some displaced individuals.

Summary

The four demonstration projects discussed in this chapter have the common purpose of quantitatively assessing the labor market effectiveness for displaced workers of retraining programs. These programs include different mixes of three reemployment services—JSA, CT, and OJT. Although they have a common objective, the projects differ considerably in terms of geographic location, experimental design, and the target populations of displaced workers served. This summary section attempts to pull together the plethora of net impact estimates reported for the different demonstrations by asking what light the results can shed on the four policy questions posed in chapter 1.

Beginning with the issue of whether some types of training work better than others, the Buffalo, Texas WAD, and New Jersey projects are unanimous in indicating that JSA services have the intended effect on a variety of labor market outcomes. These include earnings, placement and employment rates, and amount of UI benefits. Given the relatively low cost per worker of JSA, this evidence suggests also that JSA services are cost effective.

For the other reemployment services, evidence gathered for all four demonstrations indicates that CT fails to have a sizable incremental effect on earnings, employment, and UI benefits above that of JSA-only. It certainly does not appear to be the case that the additional effect of CT is large enough to compensate for the higher cost of CT services. The authors of the major evaluation reports offer a number of caveats for their findings including the difficulty of drawing reliable inferences from small sample sizes, the problem that program participants undergoing skill training have relatively little time left to receive placement assistance (given demonstration periods of fixed length), the scarcity of training providers capable of putting together high-quality, short-duration training courses on short notice, and the possibility that the classroom training provided is either not saleable in the local labor market or not of particular interest to the client population.

Regarding on-the-job training, the Buffalo project is probably the only one of the four demonstrations with enough participants placed in OJT slots to provide reasonably reliable estimates of the net impact of OJT programs. Contrary to the CETA results discussed in chapter 2, OJT is not found to consistently have a positive effect on earnings for Buffalo trainees. Nor does it have much of an effect on employment rates. Since OJT was primarily used in the Buffalo program as a placement tool, it appears that this service was unnecessary.

The next question asked whether some groups of displaced workers benefitted more from program services than others. Probably the strongest evidence relating to differences in program effects by race or ethnicity and sex is found in the results obtained for the Texas WAD projects. In terms of earnings and employment, female participants in the two El Paso projects are found to enjoy much larger net impact estimates than males in the El Paso and Houston projects. The gender differences between program sites are even more impressive when it is recognized that a majority of male Houston participants are white, whereas female El Paso participants are largely Hispanic. Reinforcing the WAD results is evidence from the Buffalo project indicating larger effects for women than men. The Buffalo project also suggests that little difference in net impact estimates exists for blacks and whites, but that workers under age 45 benefit more from program services than do older workers.

Rather than race/ethnicity and sex differences, the results of the New Jersey Demonstration emphasize the distinction between workers with marketable skills and workers facing long-term, structural reemployment problems. In New Jersey, clerical and other white-collar workers are examples of the former group, while blue-collar workers laid off from durable goods manufacturing jobs typify the latter. In view of the Demonstration's objective of encouraging rapid reemployment through the UI system, it is not surprising that program services primarily assisted workers with marketable skills.

The third question posed in chapter 1 raises the issue of whether training, to the extent that it improves reemployment prospects at all, works by increasing post-training wages or by speeding up the reemployment process. For all program services combined, the Buffalo project permits the calculation of short-run program effects on weekly hours and average weekly earnings. The larger percentage effect on average weekly earnings than on weekly hours suggests that the Buffalo program boosted hourly wages for those reemployed during the first six post-program months. For all three of its program treatments, evidence from the New Jersey Demonstration also indicates that program participation has a small positive impact on wages for reemployed claimants.

In contrast, the more detailed quarter-by-quarter program impact estimates calculated for the Texas WAD projects and the New Jersey Demonstration raise questions about whether this short-run positive effect on wage rates persists over time. For both men and women, the time pattern of the WAD results shows that the program increased quarterly earnings in the first and second quarters, followed by gradually decaying impacts for subsequent quarters. Similar results broken down by program treatment are obtained for both employment and earnings in the New Jersey Demonstration. Thus, while the reemployment process was accelerated by program services in both cases, participants' employment opportunities appear ultimately to be no better and their wages no higher than those of the members of the control group. There is no evidence, in other words, from either the WAD projects or the New Jersey Demonstration that program services permanently increased labor productivity.

The final issue raised in chapter 1 is what should workers be trained to do? A valuable contribution of the demonstration projects discussed in this chapter is to make apparent the difficulty in a short-duration demonstration of developing solid training curricula that meet the market test of providing saleable skills. Of the four demonstrations, Downriver program planners probably paid the most attention to the problem of providing retraining in occupations expected to be in high demand. Yet, the skill training programs provided to Downriver trainees are not found to have a significant incremental effect in improving reemployment prospects above those for JSA-only recipients. The WAD projects also emphasize that one reason for low program take-up rates and modest net impact estimates is that CT curricula may not match the backgrounds and perceived needs of client workers.

NOTES

1. The other two major titles are Title II, which provides training to disadvantaged youth and adults and summer jobs to disadvantaged youth, and Title IV, which authorizes training programs directly administered by the USDOL for native Americans, seasonal and migrant workers, and veterans.

2. Services were delivered at all six sites, however, and a detailed description of program design and implementation issues for the entire demonstration is found in Corson, Maynard, and Wichita (1984).

3. Bloom and Kulik (1986: 178–79) note also that, with the exception of women in Houston, control group members were able to locate new jobs paying nearly as much as they earned in their pre-layoff jobs. Thus, it is not surprising that the main effect of the WAD program was expediting the reemployment of participants at wages comparable to what they previously earned. The authors go on to suggest that with its client population of workers who appeared to be experiencing only short-run unemployment problems, there is some question whether the WAD demonstration captured the labor market circumstances faced by truly displaced workers.

4. As will be discussed in chapter 5, the Canadian federal government recently announced a policy change that specifies a more active role in the reemployment process for the UI program in that country. As of 1990, Canada's Labour Force Development Strategy requires that 10 percent of total UI expenditures must be spent on programs to upgrade the skills of unemployed workers, as well as on maternity, child care, and older worker programs.

5. The initial test of the reemployment bonus concept in this country took the form of two controlled experiments carried out in Illinois between mid-1984 and mid-1985. In the Claimant Bonus Experiment, a random sample of new UI claimants was told that they would receive a cash bonus of $500 upon reemployment. In the Employer Bonus Experiment, another random sample of new UI claimants was instructed that, once a hiring commitment was made, the employer of each newly hired claimant would be eligible for a $500 cash bonus. In contrast to the generally statistically insignificant Employer Experiment results, Woodbury and Spiegelman (1987) find that, on average, the claimant bonus reduced UI benefits by $158 and duration of insured unemployment by 1.15 weeks, where both outcome variables are measured over the benefit year.

6. Corson et al. (1989: 266, fn. 10) discuss the differences between the Illinois and the New Jersey reemployment bonus experiments that make this comparison not quite appropriate.

4
State Retraining Programs

Beginning with MDTA in 1962 and continuing through the Economic Dislocation and Worker Adjustment Assistance Act (EDWAA) passed in 1988, chapters 2 and 3 briefly described the evolution of federal programs developed to supply displaced workers with adjustment assistance services. For most of the 1980s, however, the Reagan administration's philosophy of new federalism made the states the key intergovernmental player in developing social policy initiatives including the establishment of new employment and training programs. In a recent survey of state training programs, Stevens (1986) points out that only six states do not commit funds to subsidize programs that offer either classroom or on-the-job training.

Before looking at the details of particular state programs, it is useful to draw attention to two important features that distinguish state-funded initiatives in general from those provided by the federal government.[1] First, while only unemployed workers are currently eligible for Title III JTPA services, state programs are typically offered in addition to employed workers at risk of being permanently laid off if their skills are not upgraded. Second, many states have addressed the critical issue of what to retrain displaced workers to do by tailoring training programs to meet the needs of individual employers. This means that state programs have the economic development objective of creating new jobs, in addition to the traditional view of retraining as a human capital investment intended to raise the level of workers' skills to enable them to qualify for existing jobs. Federal programs, in contrast, generally are designed to qualify program graduates for jobs in what are anticipated to be high-demand occupations. In the case of the federally funded Downriver demonstration project, for example, chapter 3 pointed out that program planners made the explicit decision not to tailor training programs to meet firm-specific labor demands.

Table 4.1
Major Features of California's ETP and Minnesota's MEED
Programs and the Dayton Experiment

Program	Targeted workers	Services provided	Funding mechanism
California's ETP	UI recipients, recent UI exhaustees, and employed workers at risk of layoff	Payment to providers of CT and OJT to cover direct program costs. Training providers may be either the employer requesting the project or a training institution.	Diversion of UI tax revenues
Minnesota's MEED	Unemployed workers not eligible for UI or workers' compensation. Priority given to General Assistance and AFDC eligibles.	Subsidies of up to $4 per hour in wages and up to $1 per hour in fringes paid to small employers	General state tax revenues
Dayton experiment	AFDC and General Assistance recipients	Wage vouchers paid to employers in the form of either a tax credit or a direct cash payment. Vouchers equal to 50% of first-year earnings and 25% of second-year earnings.	Federally funded

The first state initiative considered in this chapter—California's Employment Training Panel (ETP)—is the largest and undoubtedly the best known of ongoing state training programs. In addition, ETP is among the few state programs for which quantitative evaluation evidence is available. The Minnesota Employment and Economic Development (MEED) program is examined next as an example of the wage-subsidy approach to training and economic development. Presented in connection with the MEED program is quantitative evidence obtained for the federally funded Dayton targeted wage-subsidy experiment. Table 4.1 highlights some of the major differences between these three programs with respect to targeted workers, the services provided, and funding mechanisms.

California's ETP

Major Program Features

Begun in January 1983, ETP receives state funding of $55 million per year to be used for retraining current UI recipients, recent UI exhaustees, and workers currently employed (and covered by the UI system) but in danger of being laid off due to changes in technology or other changes in the workplace. Individual training projects eligible for ETP funding must provide at least 100 hours of instruction consisting of either CT or OJT. Projects are initially funded for up to 18 months, with possible contract extensions for as long as two years. Since its inception, the Panel has taken pride in noting that its staff, not the employer, does the paperwork; and that when speed is important the project outline and a formal agreement can be approved in a time period as short as one month.

The Panel deals with the question of what to train workers to do by making the program almost entirely employer-driven. Employers initiate the process by proposing individual projects to the Panel. If a project is approved and a contract negotiated, the employer selects trainees according to its own specifications, sets standards for successful program completion, and approves the training curriculum if an outside training provider (e.g., a state post-secondary educational institution) is selected. The Panel reimburses employers or other training providers on a fixed-fee basis for the training costs incurred. ETP funds may not be spent to subsidize the wages paid to trainees or to pay income-maintenance allowances. Nor does ETP, as is typical of state training programs, provide support for remedial education. In return for the training subsidy and the discretion given them in all aspects of the retraining process, participating employers must make a good-faith commitment to hire or retain program graduates. Largely bypassed, therefore, is the problem that workers are trained in skills that are no longer demanded by employers.

Two unique features of ETP are its funding mechanism and its extensive use of performance-based contracting. With respect to funding, state retraining programs are typically financed by general state tax revenues. A widely discussed policy issue is whether financing options for displaced worker programs should be expanded to include the use of state UI trust funds (see, for example, Kuttner 1985). Federal law currently restricts the use of UI trust funds to financing income-maintenance benefits. As noted in connection with the New Jersey Demonstration in chapter 3, critics of the present UI system argue that to facilitate the reemployment of displaced workers, the use of UI trust funds should be expanded to finance retraining and other forms of adjustment assistance. In California, ETP is linked to the state's UI trust fund by the statutory requirement that the program is to operate so as to reduce UI expenditures by speeding up claimants' reemployment. To avoid the federal prohibition on financing retraining programs with UI trust funds, a novel strategy adopted by the California legislature was to create a separate Employment Training Fund financed by a 0.1 percent payroll tax assessed on all employers with a positive reserve in their UI account. At the same time, state employers had their regular UI tax rates reduced by 0.1 percent. The funding of ETP can thus be viewed as a diversion of a small part of regular UI tax revenues to finance training and economic development. California was in a favorable position to carry out this diversion because of a surplus in its UI trust fund. Since 1983, two states—Delaware and Washington—have followed California's example in diverting regular UI contributions to separate training and economic development funds financed by an employer payroll tax.

Turning to its contracting mechanism, ETP's enabling legislation requires that all contracts between the Panel and employers or training agencies be performance-based. Performance is defined stringently to mean that the negotiated payment per worker is withheld until trainees have completed their retraining programs, are placed in training-related jobs at wage rates stipulated in the contract, and are retained in those jobs for at least 90 days. Moreover, the jobs for which workers are trained must be good jobs in the sense that they offer long-term employment security and career potential and provide wages that are customary for the occupation and industry in the local labor market in which employment is to occur. Thus Panel funds are not spent until trainees have completed their training and are satisfactorily placed.

Table 4.2
Summary Statistics for the ETP Program, June 30, 1988

Clients served by the project	Ave. cost/ trainee	Post- training wage	Ave. hours of training[a]	% of planned expenditures	
				1985	1988
Unemployed only	$3,135	$6.68	503	52	24
Potentially dis- placed only	2,196	9.42	234	31	63
Both groups	2,273	7.57	333	17	13

Sources: ETP (1985: table 4), ETP (1987: table III-D), and ETP (1988: table III-D).
[a]Data for June 30, 1987.

Evaluation Evidence

Table 4.2 presents summary statistics for successful program graduates as reported in the most recent ETP annual report (1988) to the legislature. As might be expected, upgrading the skills of current employees potentially at risk of displacement is considerably cheaper than retraining the unemployed. The average number of hours of training for employed trainees is less than half that for unemployed trainees, while the average post-training wage for employed trainees is nearly $3.00 per hour higher than for the unemployed. It is also interesting to note that as of 1988, 63 percent of ETP expenditures is directed toward potentially displaced workers only, and another 13 percent of expenditures includes the potentially displaced as well as actual unemployed workers. This is in contrast to earlier years, such as 1985, in which over 50 percent of ETP expenditures went to projects designed for the unemployed.

Estimates of the impact of ETP on participants' earnings are reported in a recent evaluation study carried out by the Training Research Corporation of Santa Monica, California (see Moore, Wilms, and Bolus 1988). Analyzed are the records of about 3,900 individuals enrolled in ETP training programs between 1983 and 1985. About 60 percent of the trainees examined were unemployed and seeking new jobs, while the other 40 percent had enrolled in retraining to avoid layoffs. As shown in table 4.3, sampled participants are further stratified by whether they completed their training program

Table 4.3
Estimated Net Impact of the ETP Program on Annual Earnings

Initial employment status and program completion status	Pre-pro-gram	Post-pro-gram	Difference (% change)	Regression coef. (stand. error)
Unemployed:				
Completed, employed 90 days (N = 234)	$9,628	$16,912	$7,284 (76)	$3,745 (691)
Dropped out (N = 125)	9,017	9,882	865 (10)	−1,351 (684)
Completed, not employed 90 days (N = 96)	10,538	12,352	1,814 (17)	+
Employed:				
Completed, employed 90 days (N = 1,008)	21,408	27,147	5,739 (27)	1,664 (1,136)
Dropped out (N = 440)	16,354	19,106	2,752 (17)	−867 (1,178)
Completed, not employed 90 days (N = 123)	14,108	20,466	6,358 (45)	+

Source: Moore, Wilms, and Bolus (1988: tables 9, 10, and 18).
Notes: Average annual earnings are shown in the first two columns. + indicates the reference group.

and, if they had completed training, whether they stayed on the job for 90 days. For the sample as a whole, participants were predominantly male heads of households between the ages of 25 and 45. Exactly one-half were white, with Hispanics representing another 25 percent and blacks 12 percent.

In the absence of a comparison or control group of nonparticipants, the Training Research Corporation evaluation relies mainly on a pre-program/post-program comparison of labor market outcomes supplemented by comparable information on program dropouts. As discussed in chapter 2, a fundamental problem with this evaluation approach is that the program effect will be overstated if the typical pre-program dip in earnings is the result of some transitory labor market phenomenon. Looking first at participants who were initially unemployed, table 4.3 presents evidence of a rebound in average annual earnings for program dropouts; but the magnitude of the rebound ($865 or 10 percent) is dwarfed by the 76 percent increase in earnings enjoyed by program completers who stayed on the job for 90 days. Of course, this comparison is marred by the self selection inherent in the unobserved process that somehow leads some participants to complete the program while others drop out. Holding constant a number of personal and program characteristics and previous earnings, the regression results appearing in the last column show that, relative to program completers who did not stay on the job for 90 days, completers who were retained enjoyed a statistically significant increase in earnings of $3,745. On the other hand, dropping out had a significantly negative earnings impact. Accepting these estimates at face value, the estimated difference in earnings between completing training and dropping out is thus $5,096 per year, or 53 percent expressed as a percentage of average pre-program earnings.

For employed program participants, the very fact that individuals were working rather than unemployed prior to entering the program means that (1) there should be less of a upward bias due to a transitory pre-program dip in carnings, and (2) any observed pre-program/post-program earnings growth should capture to a greater extent higher wages as opposed to more stable employment.[2] Reflecting these considerations, the percentage growth in earnings is seen in table 4.3 to be much smaller for initially employed program completers (27 percent) than for initially unemployed completers (76 percent). Among the initially employed, nevertheless, earnings growth for completers exceeds that for dropouts by 10 percentage points. A rather surprising result is the 45 percent earnings growth experienced by the relatively small number of program completers who did not stay on the job for 90 days. Given their low average pre-program earnings of just $14,108, it is quite possible that these individuals went through the training program and then moved on to better paying jobs with other employers. The regression results for the initially employed again indicate sizable positive and negative effects, respectively, of program completion and dropping out. In both cases, however, the estimates are accompanied by very large standard errors indicating a wide range of possible effects among individuals.

Criticisms of ETP

The two principal concerns that have been raised about the ETP program relate to the selection of participants and the use of public funds to subsidize training costs employers might otherwise have borne. There is no question that adherence to a performance-based system for compensating training providers increases the probability that the displaced workers most likely to be selected into the program will be those least in need of skill enhancement. This problem is commonly known as "creaming." One piece of evidence suggesting that creaming does in fact occur is the Panel's own finding noted in its 1988 annual report that only 8 percent of Panel trainees had failed to complete at least 12 years of schooling (see ETP 1988: table III-F). The same statistic for the state's labor force is 27 percent. However, the report also points out that 53 percent of trainees are women compared to a workforce that is 43 percent female. Blacks and Hispanics are approximately proportionately represented among ETP trainees.

Moreover, as pointed out in table 4.2, ETP increasingly appears to be subsidizing the training by firms of their current workforces as opposed to supplying training to unemployed workers. One reason, as noted in the study by the Panel of Technology and Employment of the National Academy of Sciences (see Cyert and Mowery 1987: 152), is that the requirement that trainees be placed in jobs for 90 days prior to reimbursement discourages many potential external training providers such as community colleges from participating in the program. A consequence of the increased retraining of the employed is that ETP may be substituting public funds for the training investments employers would have made themselves in the program's absence. In this situation, there would be no net increase in the delivery of training services to workers threatened with displacement. On the assumption that large firms are better able to fund retraining than small firms, the following evidence taken from ETP's 1987 annual report on the size distribution of employers of program graduates is instructive (see ETP 1987: table II-A):

Firm size	Panel trainees	Total state employment
0–49	18%	32%
50–99	6	11
100–249	10	15
250–499	14	10
500–1000	6	9
1000+	46	23

Firm size in this table is measured by number of employees. It is clear that ETP trainees are underrepresented in the workforces of small employers and overrepresented in the workforces of quite large employers.

In defense of the Panel, two points should be brought out. First, the year 1987 marked an important transition for ETP in that, for the first time, employers' demand for training assistance exceeded the supply of available funds, forcing the rationing of funds among prospective contractors. This excess-demand situation has led the Panel to impose certain priorities on its basic operating philosophy of responding to the market demand for training. More specifically, the list of new Panel priorities includes expedited consideration given to proposals in which special employment opportunities are offered to minorities, women, the disabled, and veterans and to proposals which promise assistance to persons already laid off or in danger of layoff due to plant closures or permanent mass layoffs. In addition, the Panel has committed itself to targeting approximately 30 percent of its funds for projects retraining the unemployed; and it is conducting a special marketing outreach to small businesses and minority- and female-owned enterprises.

Second and more fundamentally, ETP should be properly viewed as an economic development program to assist both employers and workers, as opposed to strictly a jobs program to assist disadvantaged workers. In this context, a major goal of the program is to provide employers with an incentive to modernize plants and avoid layoffs by subsidizing the costs of retraining existing employees. Moreover, subsidies to large employers can be rationalized on the grounds that these firms provide jobs that pay high wages and offer career potential—that is, the kinds of jobs that are mandated by ETP's enabling legislation. From a political perspective, finally, since employers of all sizes are contributing financially to ETP, the assistance to large employers is important in maintaining overall business support for the program.

Minnesota's MEED Program

Major Program Features

While not strictly a displaced worker program, the MEED wage-subsidy program has developed in such a way that it offers a useful contrast to ETP as well as being of interest in its own right. MEED was created in 1983 by a Minnesota state legislature faced with double-digit unemployment rates coupled with a high percentage of unemployed workers who had exhausted their UI eligibility. The legislature's response in MEED was a two-year program designed to create temporary jobs in the public sector and permanent jobs in the private sector. The program was initially funded at a hefty $70 million for the July 1983 to June 1985 biennium using general tax revenues.

As originally conceived, MEED was fundamentally an emergency job creation program, with at least 60 percent of the jobs created expected to be in the public sector. The focus on public-sector job creation was due to the legislature's initial skepticism about the willingness of private employers to participate in MEED. As the program evolved, however, greater than expected participation of private employers led to a reversal in job placement objectives. By the second year of the program, 60 percent of jobs were designated to be in the private sector (a 70 percent private-sector placement rate was actually achieved); and an additional $30 million was appropriated by the legislature. MEED was made a permanent program in 1985. Currently, a minimum of 75 percent of jobs created must be in the private sector; and $27 million was appropriated for MEED in the biennium ending June 30, 1987.[3] Temporary public-sector employment is presently viewed as a method for allowing the most disadvantaged to acquire the work experience that will lead to eventual private-sector MEED placement.

The private-sector component of MEED is a wage-subsidy program. The main features of the wage subsidy can be outlined as follows:

1. Eligible job seekers are those who are unemployed and are ineligible for or have exhausted either UI benefits or workers' compensation. Priority is given to applicants eligible for General Assistance or Aid to Families with Dependent Children (AFDC) and to farm families that can demonstrate severe financial need. MEED is therefore available to assist displaced workers who have exhausted their UI eligibility, but it is not restricted to only displaced workers.

2. MEED offers employers who hire targeted workers a subsidy of up to $4 per hour in wages and up to $1 per hour in fringe benefits for a maximum of 1,040 hours over 26 weeks. The 26-week period can be extended up to one year for workers undergoing job training.

3. Participating employers are given a strong financial incentive to retain targeted workers for at least 12 months beyond the 6 months of subsidized employment. If an employee is not retained on the job beyond the initial 6 months, the employer is required to repay 70 percent of the amount received under the program. No repayment is expected, on the other hand, if targeted workers are retained one year or longer beyond the subsidy period. A prorated portion of the subsidy must be repaid for employees retained less than one year.

4. Small businesses are given priority for MEED participation.

The MEED annual report covering the July 1985 to December 1986 period indicates that 85 percent of private-sector participants were employed in unsubsidized jobs at the time of a 60-day follow-up survey after the completion of the subsidy period (see Minnesota Department of Jobs and Training 1987). Of workers in unsubsidized jobs, nearly 91 percent continued to be employed by the same firm, while about 9 percent changed employers following the subsidy period. Average unsubsidized hourly wages for the two groups were $5.37 and $6.06, respectively. Most individuals employed under MEED qualify for the full subsidy over 26 weeks. Hence, average program cost per worker is relatively high at approximately $4,680.

Contrasts with ETP

Beyond the difference in economic conditions existing at their creation, the MEED program contrasts strongly with California's ETP in three additional respects. One contrast is in underlying philosophies. ETP's philosophy is that updated skills are a prerequisite for workers to obtain or retain jobs. Thus payments made to employers are viewed as reimbursement for training expenses incurred. In contrast, the explicit philosophy of MEED is that job seekers need employment, not retraining. If jobs are available, workers will be found to fill them. From this perspective, wage subsidies are primarily viewed as a job creation device. Nevertheless, MEED-funded jobs do appear in many cases to offer training opportunities. A 1985 survey (see Rangan 1985) carried out by a coalition of state organizations, the Jobs Now Coalition, indicates that over 77 percent of participating private employers provided an affirmative answer to the question, "Did you provide any special training on- or off-the-job?"

A second difference between the two programs concerns the characteristics of workers likely to receive assistance. The earlier discussion of ETP outlined the incentive for training providers to cream in the trainee-selection process. MEED, on the other hand, targets the wage-subsidy to members of specific disadvantaged groups. A more recent 1987 Jobs Now Coalition survey (see Rode 1988) indicates, in fact, that MEED placements are disproportionately held by public assistance eligibles, women, and minorities. In particular, 54 percent of its placements during the 1985–87 biennium were public assistance eligible, 42 percent were women, and 25 percent were minorities (in a state with a total minority population of only 4 to 5 percent). MEED is also increasingly directing its job placement activity to the balance of the state (i.e., counties outside the

Minneapolis-St. Paul metropolitan area) where unemployment is disproportionately concentrated.

A final contrast deals with the mix of participating employers. As noted, relatively large California employers are more likely than smaller employers to participate in ETP. In line with MEED's legislative priorities, on the other hand, small Minnesota employers are heavily involved in the program. In its 1987 survey, the Jobs Now Coalition reports the following information on the size distribution of participating employers (see Rode 1988: table 5):

Firm size	Participating firms
5 or less	51.2%
6–20	29.9
21–50	9.7
51–99	4.8
100 or more	4.3

where firm size is measured by number of full-time employees. The really dramatic feature of these data is the heavy involvement of very small, start-up firms and the almost total noninvolvement of larger employers defined as firms with 100 or more workers. As large firms are known to pay higher wages on average than smaller firms (see, for example, Brown and Medoff 1989), the MEED wage-subsidy represents an especially large cut in labor costs to smaller employers. But even given this economic incentive favoring participation by small employers, it is interesting to note that the MEED experience runs counter to the usual finding that participation in employment subsidy programs is directly related to firm size. Using a USDOL survey of nearly 6,000 employers, Bishop and Montgomery (1986) report that both knowledge of and participation in the four targeted employment subsidy programs in operation in 1980 (the Targeted Jobs Tax Credit, the WIN tax credit, and the CETA and WIN on-the-job-training programs) are strongly and positively correlated with establishment size. The authors note, however, that the participation rates of employers, even for those knowledgeable about the programs, are very low.

The Dayton Wage-Subsidy Experiment

It is also interesting to contrast the MEED wage-subsidy program with the results of a federally funded controlled experiment carried out in Dayton, Ohio during 1980–81. As described by Burtless (1985), the purpose of the experiment was to test the effectiveness of a targeted wage-subsidy program in increasing the labor market success of disadvantaged workers defined as General Assistance and AFDC recipients. General Assistance eligibles were typically young men and women who were members of one- or two-person families in which no dependent children were present. Many were temporarily destitute. AFDC recipients were largely single women in their twenties responsible for the support of one or more dependent children.

Individuals targeted by the Dayton program were randomly assigned to either of two treatment groups or to a control group. The first treatment group received vouchers that entitled their employers, upon making a hiring commitment, to a tax credit equal to 50 percent of earnings paid during the first year of employment and 25 percent of second-year earnings. The main goal of this treatment was to inform employers of clients' eligibility for tax credits under the then-existing Targeted Jobs Tax Credit and WIN tax credit programs. Rather than a tax credit, the vouchers received by members of the second treatment group authorized their employers to receive direct cash payments equal to the same percentages of the first- and second-year earnings. The difference between the two treatments is that for employers owing no federal income taxes, the tax credit vouchers were valueless, whereas the direct rebate subsidies would probably be worth claiming. Subsidy limits for both treatment groups were $3,000 and $1,500, respectively, for the first two years of employment. Members of the treatment groups and the control group received two weeks of job search training, which were followed by six weeks of structured job search. The vouchers expired at the end of the six-week job search period.

The results of the experiment are shown in table 4.4. For the two treatment groups, only 13.0 percent of the tax credit group and 12.7 percent of the direct cash payment group found employment during

Table 4.4
Job Placement Rates in the Dayton Targeted
Wage-Subsidy Experiment

Group	No. enrolled	No. placed in jobs	Placement rate
Tax credit voucher	247	32	13.0%
Direct rebate voucher	299	38	12.7
Control	262	54	20.6

Source: Burtless (1985: table 1).

the eight weeks of the experiment. Thus the direct cash payments did not increase labor market success relative to the tax credits. More important, the placement rates of both treatment groups were *lower* than the 20.6 percent rate obtained by the control group. Rather than improving the employment prospects of targeted workers, it appears that the primary use of the vouchers by Dayton employers was as a labor market signal of potentially poor job performance. This explanation would account for both the lower placement rates observed for the treatment groups and the failure of the different subsidy payment mechanisms to make a difference. The disquieting implication of the experiment for wage-subsidy policies is that vouchers appear to have a stigmatizing effect in the sense that rather than easing the placement of target groups, the vouchers provide information which employers used to discriminate against the disadvantaged.

It is also of interest to note that of the 70 voucher holders who found employment, only 19, or little more than one-quarter, were employed by firms that requested certification for payment of the wage-subsidy. Burtless speculates that the 73 percent of employers who did not request payment may have considered the subsidies too small to justify the expense of filing for them. On the other hand, participants who succeeded in finding jobs may have refrained from telling employers that they were covered by a wage-subsidy program, reasoning (correctly) that the information conveyed by the voucher would not increase their chance of finding employment. O'Neill (1982) also observes that the low utilization rates for subsidy programs that are narrowly targeted to particular socioeconomic groups may occur because targeted individuals who apply for jobs choose not to reveal to potential employers their membership in a target group.

Assessing MEED's Impact

Burtless's evaluation of the Dayton experiment and the historically low take-up rates for targeted wage-subsidies leave little room for optimism regarding the potential of these programs. MEED's record to date leads to a more positive conclusion. In particular, MEED appears to have been enthusiastically received by Minnesota employers, particularly small and relatively new businesses, despite the priority given to hiring hard-to-employ target groups. This is indicated by the shift in the program's emphasis toward private-sector job creation, its continued funding during the economic recovery following the 1981–82 recession, and surveys describing a high degree of employer satisfaction with MEED.

The reasons for the difference in employers' reactions to the Dayton and MEED programs can only be speculated upon. Nevertheless, it is clear that MEED officials, like those of California's ETP program, recognize that it is critical to retain the support of the business community. From this perspective, the following considerations may play a role in MEED's comparative success.

1. MEED is promoted as a program to assist Minnesota's small businesses to grow and diversify. That is, MEED is sold as an economic development tool rather than as a government program to assist the unemployed and disadvantaged. In this connection, the 1987 Jobs Now Coalition survey (see Rode 1988) points out that 81 percent of surveyed employers responded affirmatively to a question that asked whether MEED enabled them to expand their production or scale of operations, 60 percent noted that the wage subsidy made it possible for them to invest in new capital equipment, and 54 percent stated that MEED made it possible to diversify into new areas. Among firms that reported expansion of their workforces, 56 percent indicated that they would not have been able to create new jobs without MEED assistance, and another 4 percent suggested that their

expansion would have been delayed without the program. A further breakdown of these data suggests that MEED assistance is particularly beneficial to the growth of very small and new businesses. The same survey indicates, finally, that 86 percent of responding employers stated that they were "very satisfied" with their MEED employees, and only 23 percent mentioned that the subsidy failed to improve the performance of their business.

2. MEED officials have taken pains to keep their rules simple and administrative overhead low. The 1987 Jobs Now Coalition survey reports that 92 percent of responding employers felt that they were able to fill their jobs with a minimum of red tape, and 94 percent stated that they found the rules easy to understand. Both of these considerations are consistent with the policy conclusion reached by Bishop and Montgomery (1986) that the rate of employer usage of employment subsidy programs can be increased by vigorous promotion by local administrators and by keeping the costs of participation as low as possible.

Most state-funded training programs are like the ETP program in imposing few constraints on employers in their selection of trainees. The MEED program demonstrates that it is possible to walk the fine line between targeting assistance to particular groups of disadvantaged workers while at the same time enjoying widespread business support.

Summary

Although state-funded retraining initiatives are in operation in virtually every state, state legislators have generally not opted to devote scarce resources to funding quantitative program evaluation analyses. One of the few exceptions to this statement is the evaluation of California's ETP program described in this chapter, and even this evaluation is flawed by the absence of a comparison group of nonparticipants. The general unavailability of evaluation evidence severely limits the information that state programs can provide on the first three of the four research question posed in chapter 1, namely, the issues of whether some types of training work better than others, whether some groups of workers benefit more from training than others, and whether effective training programs operate by increasing wages rates as well as by accelerating reemployment. Fortunately, however, the design of various state programs provides considerable insight into the fourth research question of what to train workers to do.

State-funded retraining programs are typically more tailored to meet the needs of individuals employers than federal programs, and this chapter focused attention on employer involvement in the ETP program and the program's stringent performance standards. California employers are encouraged to propose individual retraining projects for ETP funding. If a project is approved and a contract negotiated, the employer selects trainees according to its own specification, sets standards for successful program completion, and approves the training curriculum if an outside training provider is used. ETP's performance standards permit training providers to be reimbursed for training expenses only for those trainees who successfully complete the program and are placed in training-related jobs at stipulated wages and are retained in those jobs for at least 90 days.

Allowing employers to participate in trainee selection and the use of performance-based contracting clearly should contribute to strong program performance in terms of job placement, and the preliminary pre-program/post-program evaluation of ETP indicates a sizable program effect on annual earnings. Nevertheless, downside factors associated with the ETP approach are an increased likelihood that training providers will select those eligible workers least in need of retraining and the strong incentive given employers to retrain current employees, as opposed to offering training to unemployed workers.

In this context, the design and operation of Minnesota's MEED targeted wage-subsidy program is instructive. Despite an absence of quantitative evaluation evidence, available qualitative measures of program success for MEED suggest that it is possible to target assistance to the hard-to-employ and still enjoy widespread business support, especially the support of small businessmen. In particular, Minnesota program officials appear to have successfully overcome the stigma associated by employers with program vouchers in the federally funded Dayton targeted wage-subsidy experiment.

NOTES

1. More information on the broad range of proposed and ongoing state initiatives to assist displaced workers is found in Leigh (1989). In addition to vocational training and job search assistance, these initiatives include wage subsidies, reemployment bonuses, rapid-response team programs, enterprise zones, employee buy-one assistance, and unemployed entrepreneur programs.

2. Moore, Wilms, and Bolus (1988: tables 11 and 12) report for initially unemployed training completers that the average annual number of weeks unemployed fell from 6.2 weeks before training to 2.7 weeks after training. For initially employed training completers, the comparable change is from 2.4 weeks before training to 1.2 weeks after training.

3. MEED was appropriated $18 million for the July 1, 1987 to December 31, 1988 fiscal year. Indicating a possible phasing out of the program, just $4 million has been appropriated for July 1, 1989 to June 30, 1990.

5
Canadian Training Programs

For over 60 years, the Canadian government has provided unemployed workers with employment information and job placement services delivered through a joint federal-provincial network of Canada Employment Centres. With the passage of the Adult Occupational Training (AOT) Act in 1966, the federal government initiated, in addition, a series of training programs intended to improve the reemployment prospects of adult workers. AOT programs included the purchase of classroom training from community colleges and other training institutions under the Canadian Manpower Training Program (CMTP) and on-the-job training purchased from private-sector employers under the Canadian Manpower Industrial Training Program (CMITP).

Following a critical evaluation of these programs in 1981 (the "Dodge Report"), the AOT Act was replaced by the National Training Act (NTA) passed in 1982. While continuing the earlier legislation's emphasis on increasing the earnings and employment potential of individual workers, the central objective of the NTA was to provide vocational training in order to better meet the skill requirements of a changing Canadian economy. Major component programs of the NTA were (1) the National Institutional Training Program, which continued the CMTP's focus on formal classroom training, (2) the National Industrial Training Program, which emphasized OJT, and (3) the Skills Growth Fund, which was intended to expand the capacity of the Canadian economy to train workers for jobs in shortage occupations. The National Institutional Training Program was by far the largest of the three NTA programs.

During the fall of 1984, a change in administrations at the federal level resulted in a comprehensive review of all federal labor market policies. The outcome of this review was the establishment in 1985 of an umbrella program called the Canadian Jobs Strategy (CJS).

This chapter begins with a brief overview of the component programs of the CJS that relate to adjustment problems faced by displaced workers. This section is followed by discussions of two major quantitative evaluations of Canadian displaced worker programs. Considered first is a 1985 evaluation, carried out by Abt Associates of Canada, of CT programs funded by the National Institutional Training Program. Then the results of a 1981 evaluation of CMITP-funded OJT programs are examined. This second evaluation was conducted by the Program Evaluation Branch of Employment and Immigration Canada (EIC). Also briefly discussed in connection with the CMITP evaluation are results from an evaluation of the Youth Training Option program.

The Canadian Jobs Strategy

As summarized in table 5.1, the CJS consists of six component programs each of which is designed to meet the adjustment assistance needs of a particular client group—workers, employers, or communities. Like the state-funded programs discussed in chapter 4, CJS retraining assistance is available to employed workers at risk of being laid off if their skills are not upgraded, as well as to already unemployed workers. In addition, CJS programs emphasize involvement by private-sector employers at the local level. The three CJS programs that appear to be most relevant to the needs of Canadian displaced workers are Job Development, Skill Investment, and Community Futures.[1]

Job Development

This CJS program is designed to provide training and practical work experience for the long-term unemployed defined as individuals out of work 24 of the last 30 weeks who are referred to the program through a Canada Employment Centre. Funding both classroom training and on-the-job training, the Job Development program is seen in table 5.1 to be the largest of the six programs in terms of 1986–87 expenditures and number of participants. Job Development

Table 5.1
Component Programs of the Canadian Jobs Strategy

Program name	Description	1986–87 expenditures ($millions)	1986–87 participants (000s)
Skill Shortages	Provides subsidies to employers that train workers in high-demand skills that may be in short supply.	182.2	70.9
Skill Investment	Assists experienced workers to retain their jobs by updating their skills. Five options are available.	41.2	17.8
Job Entry	Assists youth in making the transition from school to work and women having difficulty re-entering the labor market after an absence from the workforce.	402.9	149.0
Job Development	Assists the reemployment of the long-term unemployed.	768.7	176.2
Community Futures	Assists single-industry communities hit by plant closings and mass layoffs.	63.5	3.1
Innovations	Funds pilot projects and demonstration projects.	14.8	—

Source: EIC (1988: 48–49 and 64–65).

training takes place in two forms. First, employers are assisted in developing projects that create three or more jobs lasting between 16 and 52 weeks. Second, for the long-term unemployed who have particular employment disadvantages due to social or cultural barriers, assistance is provided to employers who develop individual-specific training slots lasting up to 52 weeks. Employers participating in either Job Development component are eligible to receive (1) up to 60 percent of wages paid subject to a cap of $7.50 per hour with a weekly maximum of $300 per participant (up to 100 percent of wages for nonprofit employers), (2) up to $8 per participant training hour to cover the direct costs of CT provided either on-site or off-site at a community college or another recognized training institution, and (3) payment to cover the salaries received by administrative staff. In addition, employers who purchase special equipment or make structural renovations to the workplace to accommodate physically disabled employees can receive up to $10,000 per participant to defray these costs.

Skill Investment

Rather than waiting to intervene until after workers have been laid off, the Skill Investment program is designed to provide classroom and on-the-job training to enable experienced workers to retain their jobs through skill upgrading. Client groups are presented with five options. First, the Retraining option helps to pay wages and training costs for small businesses faced with rapid technological and market change. (Small businesses are defined as firms with less than 100 employees.) Employers providing OJT are eligible to receive a wage subsidy of up to 60 percent of wages subject to ceilings per worker of $7.50 per hour and $300 per week. For providing CT opportunities, employers are eligible to receive up to $20 per hour for each participant training hour. The minimum length of training is 80 hours, and agreements with the Skill Investment program can last up to three years. Special funds are also available to defray the costs of assisting the physically disabled.

The Continuing Employment option is directed to workers who are in danger of losing or who have lost their jobs within the past four months because of market or technological change. Current and new employers who employ participating workers are eligible to receive the same financial support as that provided under the Retraining option. For the same target group of workers, a third option—Relocation and Travel Assistance—offers up to $5,000 to meet the relocation and travel assistance requirements of program participants.

The fourth option—Work Sharing—attempts to avert temporary layoffs and to cushion the impact of permanent layoffs by providing partial compensation for the reduced earnings that accompany a shorter workweek. Under this voluntary program, employers continue to pay for regular hours worked, but participating workers receive UI benefits for time not worked up to a total of three days per week. These Work Sharing days may be used for training, with employers reimbursed for a major portion of direct training costs. Work Sharing agreements are normally expected to be in effect for 6 to 26 weeks.

Finally, the Training Trust Fund option encourages unions and employee associations to combine with employers in establishing trust funds intended to finance workers' future training needs. Under agreements that can last up to three years, the Canadian federal government will supplement the trust funds by 50 percent of total contributions in the first year and 33⅓ percent of total contributions in the second and third years. A similar concept proposed but not yet implemented in this country is the Individual Training Accounts (ITA) proposal. As described by the Office of Technology Assessment (1986: 265–67), the basic idea underlying the ITA concept is the establishment of a fund privately financed by workers, employers, or both workers and employers that can be drawn upon to pay for additional educational or training investments. Workers who have lost their jobs or received notice of layoff would be eligible to withdraw funds from their training accounts to assist them in making necessary transitions to new jobs or careers.

Community Futures

Instead of targeting on either workers or employers, this CJS program is designed to assist nonmetropolitan, often one-industry communities that have been hard hit by a plant closing or mass permanent layoff. The program revolves around Community Futures Committees composed of local workers, employers, and government officials. Once established, these committees can choose from among the following options offered under the program:

1. Business Development Centres, which provide technical and advisory services to small businesses as well as loans of up to $75,000 per firm.

2. Income-maintenance support of $180 per week for one year to enable unemployed workers to start their own small businesses.[2]

3. Assistance to employed, self-employed, and unemployed individuals to cover the direct costs of classroom training in approved training institutions.

4. Relocation and travel assistance to enable individuals or groups of workers to move to jobs elsewhere.

5. Community Initiative Funds, which will match funds obtained from other sources to finance local projects designed to generate new permanent jobs. These options are available to Community Futures Committees for up to five years.

Beyond the component programs of the CJS, an interesting policy change announced by the EIC in April 1989 is the creation of a new plan, the Labour Force Development Strategy, to change the allocation of Canadian UI expenditures. As in the U.S., the traditional role of Canada's UI program is the essentially passive one of providing temporary income support to individuals who are involuntarily out of work. A very small percentage of total UI expenditures has been devoted to training and upgrading workers' skills. Beginning in 1990, the new plan calls for 10 percent of the UI program's total expenditures (or $1.3 billion) to be redirected to a more active response to the needs of the unemployed. Some $800 million of this amount will be allocated to upgrading job skills; and about $500 million will go to improving UI benefits for maternity, sickness, and parental leave, as well as for workers over the age of 65 (EIC: 1989).

The NITP Evaluation

As noted at the beginning of this chapter, the National Institutional Training Program (NITP) was created in 1982 to fund CT slots in specific vocational courses offered by public and private vocational centers, technical institutes, and community colleges. Channeling training purchases primarily through the individual provinces, training courses supported by the NITP were generally under 52 weeks in length and did not lead to a diploma or degree. Also funded, in addition to the direct costs of training, was income-maintenance support for trainees. Canadian Employment Centres were given the task of enrolling and referring candidates to the program.

The NITP included the following component programs: (1) Skill Training, (2) Language Training, (3) Basic Training for Skill Development (BTSD), (4) Apprenticeship Training, (5) Job Readiness Training, (6) Work Adjustment Training, and (7) Occupational Orientation. BTSD courses were designed to upgrade basic skills in mathematics and communications so that participants could meet the academic requirements for entry into the Skill Training program or to proceed on to employment.[3] Skill Training courses were designed either to provide entry-level skills in a particular occupation or to upgrade or update the occupation-specific skills a worker already possessed. The 1985 program evaluation reported in Robinson et al. (1985) examines specifically the Skill Training and BTSD programs. NITP is thus unique among the projects and programs examined in this study in that net impact estimates are available for a remedial education program. For both NITP programs analyzed, the twofold objective of the evaluation is (1) to determine the impact of institutional training on the employability and earnings of trainees, and (2) to examine the impact of institutional training on meeting the skill needs of the economy.

An interesting feature of the NITP evaluation is that it provides a comparison of program impact estimates obtained using pre- and post-training data on labor market outcomes for participants with program impacts estimated using a comparison sample of nonparticipants. The participant sample includes about 1,500 Skill Training trainees and about 500 BTSD trainees who finished training courses in 1983–84. About 30 percent of all Skill trainees were women, while nearly half of all BTSD trainees were female. For both programs, more than three-quarters of all trainees were unemployed prior to training, and most trainees were in the 20–44 age bracket. Pre-program data for the sample of participants were obtained from administrative records, and a follow-up telephone survey conducted 12 months after the completion of training provided post-training information.

Construction of the comparison samples began with the drawing of 2,000 nonparticipants matched to the characteristics of individuals in the Skill Training and BTSD participant samples. Matching criteria used in drawing the comparison samples include age, sex, province, years in the labor force, proportion of time employed and gross earnings in the year before training, and proportion of time employed and average annual gross earnings, 1972 to training start. The next step was to obtain addresses or telephone numbers so that the follow-up survey could be administered. Difficulties in making contact with many of the matched nonparticipants resulted in quite small comparison groups numbering just 55 individuals for the BTSC program and 165 individuals for the Skill Training program. The small size of the comparison samples relative to the size of the participant samples decreases the efficiency of the net impact estimates provided in the Robinson *et al.* report.

Beginning with the empirical results for the Skill Training program, the top half of table 5.2 indicates that in comparison to pre-program levels, participants' annual earnings and time employed as a fraction of time in the labor force increased substantially. The percentage increases in these two outcome measures are roughly offsetting, so that the rise in average weekly earnings expressed as a percentage of pre-program earnings is a moderate 5.3 percent. Both earnings variables are deflated to 1981 dollars to abstract from the effect of inflation. For the comparison group of nonparticipants, sizable increases in the employment ratio and in annual earnings are also observed, reflecting Canada's strong recovery from its worst postwar recession in 1981–82. While the observed employment and earnings gains for nonparticipants are not as large as for participants, the percentage increase in weekly wages of 7.7 percent is slightly higher.

The regression coefficient estimates shown in the last column of the table measure program impacts after netting out improvements in the outcome measures that occurred for nonparticipants and control-

Table 5.2
Net Impact Estimates for the NITP, Skill Training and BTSD Programs

Outcome measure	Participants			Comparison Group			Regression coef. (t-statistic)
	Year before training	Post-training	Difference (% change)	Year before training	Post-training	Difference (% change)	
			Skill Training				
Time employed/time in LF	41%	66%	25% (61.0)	54%	65%	11% (20.4)	-0.27 (-1.88)
Time employed/ calendar time							0.31 (2.07)
Ave. weekly wage	$262	$276	$14 (5.3)	$299	$322	$23 (7.7)	-17.87 (-1.09)
Annual earnings	$6,573	$10,195	$3,622 (55.1)	$7,248	$9,947	$2,699 (37.2)	762.98 (1.10)
			BTSD				
Time employed/time in LF	26%	54%	28% (107.7)	55%	65%	10% (18.2)	0.80 (-4.00)
Time employed/ calendar time							-0.38 (-1.96)
Ave. weekly wage	$178	$209	$31 (17.4)	$305	$302	-$3 (-1.0)	-49.27 (-3.24)
Annual earnings	$3,912	$6,590	$2,678 (68.5)	$6,460	$9,350	$2,890 (44.7)	-1,408.57 (-2.05)

Source: For Skill Training, Robinson et al. (1985: exhibits V-14 through V-18). For BTSD Robinson et al. (1985: exhibits V-19 through V-23).
Note: Weekly wages and annual earnings are converted to 1981 dollars using the Consumer Price Index.

ling for the effects of a number of personal characteristics and pre-training labor market variables. No attempt was made to control for self-selection bias. The regression results show that Skill Training fails to have a statistically significant effect on either earnings measure, while program participation does appear to increase the employment-to-calendar-time ratio but to decrease the employment-to-labor-force-time ratio. The suggestion is that program participation increases the extent of labor force participation. In total, these discouraging results for the Skill Training program reinforce the similar findings obtained for classroom training programs in the U.S. demonstration projects.

The interpretation of comparable empirical results for BTSD trainees is clouded by the fact that the BTSD program was not necessarily intended to prepare workers for immediate employment and the small size of the comparison sample. Despite these caveats, the pre-program/post-training comparisons shown in the lower half of table 5.2 indicate even larger percentage increases for BTSD trainees in each of the three outcome measures than those reported for Skill Training participants. The percentage increases for BTSD trainees are also considerably larger than those for the comparison sample. Nevertheless, the results of the regression analysis suggest that BTSD training significantly *decreases* weekly and annual earnings as well as both employment measures. It should be noted from the table that the wages and annual earnings of nonparticipants are on average much higher than the wages and annual earnings of BTSD trainees in both the pre-training and post-training periods. Despite the attempt to match members of the comparison group to sample members, it appears that in addition to its small size, the comparison group contains relatively few individuals with characteristics like those of BTSD trainees.

In view of the NITP's objective of meeting the skill requirements of the Canadian economy, it is also interesting to briefly review the analysis of the occupational distribution of training provided in the Abt Associates report. The analysis is limited to only Skill Training participants; and the three indicators of skill shortages applied in the analysis are (1) occupations in short supply as determined by the

EIC's Program Evaluation Branch, (2) occupations considered to be of national importance, and (3) occupations with the highest expected growth rates. The evidence presented is mixed. With respect to the first indicator, fewer than 11 percent of trainees were in courses supplying training in what are classified as shortage occupations. Conversely, about 65 percent of trainees were trained in "surplus" occupations. As measured by the other two indicators, however, there appears to be a substantial degree of targeting to shortage occupations. One further, but related, point of interest is that the Abt Associates analysis of data on the occupation of post-training employment indicates that the fraction of trainees who actually used their training on the job is quite low.

The CMITP Evaluation

In contrast to the NITP's emphasis on formal classroom training provided through Canada's educational infrastructure, the purpose of the earlier Canadian Manpower Industrial Training Program (CMITP) was to encourage employers to provide skill training (termed "industrial" training) either in a classroom setting or on the job. Eligible employers were reimbursed, either in whole or in part, for the direct training expenses incurred and for a fraction of trainees' wages. Since OJT was by far the more important source of training, however,[4] the CMITP was basically a wage-subsidy program with the level of the wage-subsidy hinging on the pre-program employment status of the trainee. Maximum subsidies were 40 percent, 60 percent, and 85 percent, respectively, for employed, unemployed, and special needs trainees. (Special needs trainees include persons who are physically or mentally handicapped, natives, or unable to find work due to social barriers such as alcoholism or police records.)

The Net Impact Analysis

The internal evaluation carried out by the Program Evaluation Branch of the EIC (1981) uses pre- and post-program data on the approximately 83,000 individuals trained during the 1978–79 period.

Table 5.3
Comparison of Pre- and Post-Program Weekly Wages for the CMITP

Program completion status and trainee category	Pre-program	Post-program	% change
Program completers:			
Employed	$256	$322	25.8
Unemployed	164	234	42.7
Special needs	142	200	40.8
Dropouts:			
Employed	189	277	46.6
Unemployed	167	236	41.3
Special needs	144	211	46.5

Source: EIC (1981: table 5.2).

Employed trainees represented the largest group of trainees (48 percent) and special needs trainees the smallest (8 percent). About 72 percent of all trainees were men. Relative to the sample of NITP participants, the most noticeable characteristic of CMITP trainees is their youth. Fully 51 percent of all trainees fell into the 14–24 age bracket. Administrative records provided pre-program information for the 12 months prior to training, and a 12-month follow-up survey was used to supply post-program data. The training programs themselves varied in length by trainee category. Special needs trainees received, on average, the longest training (674 hours), followed in order by unemployed trainees (586 hours) and employed trainees (319 hours). Over half of the employed trainees were enrolled in short duration training of less than 160 hours.

In the absence of an externally selected comparison group, the only available evaluation methodology for the CMITP is a pre-program/post-program comparison of average weekly wages for program completers and dropouts. Data reported in the EIC evaluation on average hours worked per week indicates very little change before and after training, making it reasonable to treat growth in weekly earnings as gains in hourly wage rates. The percentage changes shown in table 5.3 for program completers indicate that both initially unemployed and special need trainees benefited from the program to a greater extent than did initially employed trainees. As compared to program dropouts, however, there is no evidence for any of the three trainee categories that program completion had a positive payoff expressed in terms of wage gains. Taken at face value, this result supports a similar finding obtained for OJT in the Buffalo Dislocated Worker Demonstration Project (see chapter 3). It should be emphasized, however, that the decision to drop out is not exogenously determined, so there is good reason to expect that the effect of program completion may be understated. For example, it might be the case that trainees with above-average levels of ability are able to cut short their training program by locating a high-paying job with an alternative employer, thus biasing downward the measured effect of training.

Data on Participating Employers

The EIC evaluation also provides data on participating employers collected in a separate follow-up survey. Panel A of table 5.4 indicates that very small firms (i.e., those employing less than 10 workers) trained about 46 percent of both unemployed and special needs trainees as opposed to just 16 percent of employed trainees. On the other hand, firms in the two largest size categories (100–499 employees and 500 and more employees) trained nearly 60 percent of employed participants but only 19 percent and 12 percent, respectively, of unemployed and special needs trainees. These results parallel the findings discussed in chapter 4 for the California ETP and Minnesota MEED initiatives that large employers are disproportionately likely to participate in programs providing training to existing employees, while very small employers have a greater propensity to participate in programs directed at unemployed workers.

Panel B of table 5.4 provides a limited amount of information on the issue raised in chapter 4 of whether government-sponsored retraining programs generate a net increase in the delivery of training services. In exploring this issue, the EIC employer follow-up survey posed several questions including the three reported in the table. The three questions were worded as follows:

> Without the financial support of the program it would have been impossible for your firm to provide this training.

> Excluding this industrial training contract, has your firm provided training to its employees before?
>
> In the absence of the CMITP, what alternative course of action would your firm have followed to acquire qualified workers in the training occupation? [Seven possible responses followed, and the respondent for each employer was to check only the single most important one.]

Employers' answers to the first two questions indicate that the net impact of CMITP on training opportunities depends strongly on firm size. Large firms of 500 or more employees were quite likely to have an ongoing training program, and only about one-quarter of these firms stated that the financial assistance of the program was necessary for them to supply training to employees. At the other extreme, fully 28 percent of very small firms had no experience providing training services before CMITP, and 65 percent of these firms reported that government financial assistance was essential for implementing a training program.

The interpretation of responses to the final question asking about employer training behavior in the absence of the CMITP is complicated by the availability of financial assistance to employers who are retraining existing employees as well as to employers hiring and training new employees. Of the four response options shown, the two that relate to employers responding to the program by expanding the level of their operations are the easiest to interpret and, at the same time, reinforce the impression that the CMITP has the largest net impact for small firms. Table 5.4 indicates that over 46 percent of firms in the largest size category stated that they would have provided the same hours of training to the same number of employees in the absence of the program, while only 23 percent of the very small firms reported that their behavior would have been unchanged in this way. Conversely, only 5 percent of the largest firms stated that they would not have hired and trained new workers in the program's absence, in contrast to 26 percent of very small firms.

Using the employer survey data, Simpson (1984) presents an econometric analysis which sheds some additional light on employers' willingness to supply industrial training and on the nature of that

Table 5.4
Effect of the CMITP on Training Opportunities,
by Size of Training Employer

	Employer size (in number of employees)				
	1–9	**10–49**	**50–99**	**100–499**	**500+**
A. Distribution of Trainees					
Employed	15.8%	18.1%	7.8%	23.5%	34.8%
Unemployed	45.9	28.4	7.0	10.5	8.2
Special needs	46.4	33.6	7.9	6.2	5.9
B. Net Impact on Training					
Financial aid was essential to provide training	65.4	58.5	53.5	42.0	24.5
Employer never provided training before	28.4	15.4	10.4	10.7	8.3
In the absence of the program the employer would[a]					
Have provided the same training to the same no. of employees	23.0	23.9	26.0	29.5	46.4
Have provided fewer hours of training or trained fewer workers	26.4	28.9	34.7	30.8	27.4
Not have expanded employment and training opportunities	25.7	22.4	16.4	14.0	5.3
Have hired an already qualified employee	19.0	18.5	19.4	15.1	12.0

Source: EIC (1981: tables 3.3 and 7.7 and appendix tables E.1 and E.2).
[a]Columns do not sum vertically to 100 percent because of the omission of an open-ended "other" response and of the response that the absence of the program would have no effect on training, recruiting qualified workers, or level of the firm's operation.

training. His key results are summarized in table 5.5, where establishment size is measured by gross revenue in millions of dollars, and CMITP assistance is captured by a dummy variable measuring whether or not the employer accepted the government wage-subsidy. The dependent variable is duration in months of industrial nonapprenticeship training programs. Since months of industrial training

Table 5.5
**Estimated Impacts of Establishment Size and CMITP Assistance on
Length of Company Training Programs**

Explanatory variable	All programs	Specific training	General training
Establishment size	0.0221*	0.0246*	−0.0047
CMITP assistance	2.482*	3.038*	−0.164

Source: Simpson (1984: Table 2).
Notes: Estimates shown are Tobit slope estimates calculated using Tobit regression coefficients and evaluating the explanatory variables at their means. *signifies that the underlying Tobit regression coefficient is significant at the 5 percent level.

can be zero or positive but not negative, Simpson uses the Tobit regression technique to obtain unbiased parameter estimates for an extensive list of explanatory variables. As the Tobit model is nonlinear, slope estimates analogous to ordinary least squares coefficient estimates are calculated using the Tobit parameter estimates and evaluating all the explanatory variables at their means.

Looking at the first column of table 5.5, the significantly positive slope estimate for establishment size reinforces the conclusion that larger employers are more likely to provide training services. Holding constant the effect of size, acceptance of the CMITP wage-subsidy increases length of training programs by about two and one-half months on average. Unfortunately, Simpson's results do not differentiate between programs directed at unemployed workers and those intended to upgrade the skills of existing employees.

The second and third columns of table 5.5 attempt to pin down the nature of the training provided. Distinguishing specific from general training by employers' answers to a question asking whether vacancies in a particular occupation might be filled by hiring outside personnel with the required skills, firm size is seen to be positively associated with specific but not general training. Similarly, receipt of government assistance increases specific training by three months on average, but it has no appreciable effect on general training. The latter result is anticipated since human capital theory suggests that general training, since it is transferable between employers, will be fully paid for by trainees in the form of reduced wages. Thus, subsidies to employers are expected to be effective only in cases where workers are unable to finance general training investments because of wage floors. On the other hand, the theory predicts that employers will share in the cost of specific training, so that a wage-subsidy program can potentially make a difference in available training opportunities.

The YTO Evaluation

One other, more recent, Canadian evaluation study that should be briefly mentioned is the EIC (1987) analysis of the Youth Training Option (YTO) of the Job Entry program. As noted in table 5.1, Job Entry is the component of the CJS designed to assist noncollege-bound youth in making the transition from school to work. The EIC evaluation examines the YTO program as it existed during its pilot project phase, which lasted from September 1984 to December 1985. During this period, a total of 4,320 individuals began training in YTO projects. Trainees were about equally divided by sex and about 85 percent were between the ages of 18 and 21. Nearly 90 percent of trainees were unemployed immediately prior to program entry.

For the purpose of this monograph, the most noteworthy feature of the YTO is its goal of involving private-sector employers in actual program delivery. YTO supplied a combined program of formal classroom training coupled with on-the-job training furnished in an operating business termed a "training place host." The focal point of the program was the "managing coordinator" who, under contract to the EIC, was responsible for developing and implementing proposals, arranging the off-site CT programs, and securing training place hosts to provide OJT. In addition, the managing coordinator was in charge of recruiting, selecting, and placing trainees and monitoring their progress through the program. Managing coordinators could be private businesses or business-oriented groups such as Chambers of Commerce, government departments or agencies, school boards or schools, and community-oriented nonprofit organizations.

In an effort to isolate the effect of the private-sector involvement in the program, the EIC's evaluation strategy compares the labor market performance of YTO trainees with that of a comparison group of NITP participants. As described earlier in this chapter, NITP featured very little employer participation since it was designed to supply classroom training through Canada's existing educational infrastructure. Using samples of about 2,500 YTO trainees and about 2,000 NITP trainees, the average employment rate for YTO trainees is found to rise from 33.1 percent in the 12-month pre-training period to 69.8 percent in the 4-month post-training period. This 36.7 percentage point increase dwarfs the 7.7 percent point increase measured over the same period for NITP participants. Making use of a regression framework to control for other measured characteristics of trainees, YTO participants are found to have experienced post-program employment rates 16 percentage points higher than NITP trainees.

Summary

This chapter began by providing an overview of the broad range of services offered displaced workers through the Canadian Jobs Strategy. These services, like the state programs discussed in chapter 4, are available to employed workers at risk of layoff as well as to already unemployed workers. In addition to standard CT and OJT services directed to workers and employers, the Community Futures program of the CJS also provides a variety of forms of assistance to small communities hard hit by a plant closure or mass layoff.

The remainder of the chapter focused on the available evaluations of two major Canadian displaced worker programs. Regarding the labor market effectiveness of classroom and on-the-job training, these evaluations generally support the conclusions reached in chapter 3 for the U.S. demonstration projects. Evidence for the NITP's Skill Training component using a comparison group of nonparticipants indicates that CT does not have a statistically significant impact on either weekly wages or annual earnings. Similarly, the pre-program/post-program comparison available for evaluating the CMITP fails to indicate for any of the three categories of workers considered (employed, unemployed, or special needs) that completion of an OJT program increased wages above the wage gains enjoyed by program dropouts.

A unique feature of the NITP among the programs examined in this monograph is that it provided remedial education as well as skill training. Unfortunately, the effort to upgrade basic mathematics and communications skills in the BTSD component of the program is found to significantly decrease both earnings and employment opportunities. This result must, however, be interpreted with more than usual caution for at least two reasons. First, remedial education was not necessarily intended to prepare workers for immediate employment. Second, the appropriateness of the comparison group of nonparticipants may be questioned since, in addition to being very small, it appears to contain relatively few individuals with characteristics like those of trainees.

An employer survey included as part of the CMITP evaluation also provides evidence supporting some of the conclusions reached in chapter 4. The internal EIC evaluation of these survey data reinforces a finding for Minnesota's MEED program indicating that small employers have a substantially greater propensity than larger employers to participate in retraining initiatives directed at unemployed workers. On the other hand, large Canadian employers, like the large California employers in the ETP program, are disproportionately likely to participate in programs intended to upgrade the skills of existing employees. The CMITP employer survey data also suggest that among participating employers, it is small firms that are most likely to respond to a wage-subsidy program by generating a net increase in the delivery of training services. Although it is a training initiative directed at noncollege-bound youth rather than displaced workers, finally, the evaluation of the YTO program provides some evidence that the involvement of private-sector employers in a combined CT-OJT program can make a substantial difference in the post-program employability of participants.

NOTES

1. Later in the chapter, the Job Entry program is also discussed in connection with the evaluation of the Youth Training Option, which is a component program within Job Entry.

2. The available evidence on the effectiveness of programs in Britain and France and of a pilot project in Ohio that provide income-maintenance allowances and entrepreneurship training to unemployed workers who establish small businesses is examined in Leigh (1989: 126–31).

3. Under the Canadian Jobs Strategy established in 1985, BTSD is only provided as a prerequisite for skill training programs.

4. About 84 percent of participating employers provided training by asking trainees to do the same work as other workers or to work as helpers in teams of experienced workers.

6
Australian Training Programs

The Australian federal government has funded programs aimed specifically at assisting workers displaced by structural change since the early 1970s. The first of these programs was the Structural Adjustment Assistance (SAA) program begun in 1973 and terminated in 1976. SAA was followed by the Labour Adjustment Training Arrangements (LATA) created in 1982. Finally, the Heavy Engineering Labour Adjustment Assistance program was introduced in 1986. This chapter begins with an overview of these displaced worker programs, including a discussion of parallels between the SAA program and the U.S. Trade Adjustment Assistance program. Then the results of a 1986 evaluation of the LATA program are examined (see Ho-Trieu 1986).

Basic Elements of the Programs

The SAA Program

Table 6.1 summarizes the three Australian displaced worker programs in terms of targeted workers and the adjustment assistance services offered. During its three-year existence, the SAA program provided income-maintenance allowances to workers and proprietors of small businesses made jobless by structural changes resulting from particular federal government policy decisions. These policy decisions included a 25 percent cut in tariffs carried out in July 1973 and changes in a number of industry-specific assistance measures. Workers directly affected by these actions became eligible under SAA for six months of income-maintenance payments, with the size of the payment set equal to the individual's average wage over the previous six months subject to a cap of 1.5 times the average weekly earnings of all Australian workers.

As a policy response to trade liberalization and in its emphasis on income maintenance rather than retraining, the short history

91

Table 6.1
Australian Programs to Assist Displaced Workers

Program	Targeted workers	Program services
SAA (1973–76)	Trade-displaced workers	Income-maintenance allowances
LATA (1982–present)	Workers displaced from designated industries including steel, coal, and autos	Payment to schools for the direct costs of CT plus income-maintenance allowances paid to trainees
Heavy Engineering Labor Adjustment Assistance (1986–present)	Workers displaced in the heavy engineering industry	(1) Payment to schools for the direct costs of CT plus income-maintenance allowances paid to trainees (2) Financial assistance to employers to develop formal training programs (3) Wage-subsidy payments to employers to encourage OJT (4) Relocation assistance to workers

of the SAA program offers striking parallels to the much longer lived Trade Adjustment Assistance (TAA) program originally enacted by the U.S. Congress in 1962. TAA assistance included income-maintenance support above that provided by UI, and targeted workers were those displaced from jobs in industries adversely affected by increased foreign competition arising from the relaxation of import restrictions. To counteract the expected effect of income maintenance in lengthening unemployment spells, TAA provided job search assistance and relocation allowances to eligible displaced workers. Skill retraining was also available to assist in the replacement of specific human capital made obsolete by trade-related displacement.

For the first 12 years of TAA, a very low rate of participation reflected the program's stringent requirement that affected workers and firms demonstrate that trade liberalization led to increased imports which, in turn, were the "major" cause of reduced domestic sales and lost jobs. The Trade Act of 1974 relaxed TAA requirements making eligibility easier and providing an even more generous income support package over a longer time period. The combination of easier eligibility and improved benefits caused TAA expenditures and the number of workers served to increase rapidly over the next several years, peaking at more than $2.2 billion and over 500,000 workers in 1980. Nevertheless, very few TAA recipients received any reemployment services. Bednarzik and Orr (1984) cite a General Accounting Office study indicating that over the 1975–78 period, less than 1 percent of program participants received JSA and relocation services and less than 4 percent received skill training.

Returning to Australia's SSA, a program review was conducted in 1975 at the request of the Prime Minister, which resulted in the recommendation that SSA be discontinued. The review panel's negative recommendation was based on the following overlapping arguments (Bureau of Labour Market Research 1987: 194):

1. The special benefits to designated displaced workers reduce the mobility of those affected by structural change, thus decreasing the efficiency of the labor market.

2. Pressures on the government to extend benefits to other unemployed workers are difficult to resist.

3. Those unemployed for reasons other than the particular policy decisions or through the indirect effects of these decisions are not eligible for program assistance.

4. The determination of whether particular workers are unemployed as a result of the government's specific policy decisions is difficult and arbitrary.

For many of the same reasons, the available evaluations of TAA conclude with generally negative appraisals of the program. Neumann (1978) reports that the higher income-maintenance benefits received by trade displaced workers tended to increase unemployment duration and (for men only) post-unemployment earnings, and that training and counseling services had little effect on reemployment. Examining the post-1974 operation of TAA, Corson and Nicholson

(1981) similarly conclude that the higher wage-replacement ratio lengthened unemployment spells. But they find no appreciable effect on post-unemployment earnings. Probably the strongest result presented by Corson and Nicholson is that the liberalization of eligibility conditions in 1974 caused a dramatic shift in the composition of TAA recipients. Rather than primarily benefiting workers formerly employed in older declining industries who could not reasonably expect to be recalled to their old jobs, nearly 72 percent of TAA recipients ended their unemployment spells by returning to work for their previous employer. A reasonably high expectation of being able to return to one's old job is surely an important factor in explaining the very small percentages of recipients who made use of available reemployment services.

Congressional concern over TAA's high cost and the special treatment of program recipients whose labor market circumstances did not appear to be that different from those of regular UI recipients led to new legislation in 1981 that tightened eligibility and reduced income support payments. Authorization for TAA lapsed in 1985, but legislation passed in 1986 extended a much scaled-back version of the program for five more years. The 1986 legislation included a requirement that receipt of income support is conditional on participation in a job search program, and that workers are to be encouraged, but not required, to engage in skill training. Most recently, the Omnibus Trade and Competitiveness Act of 1988 amended both the Trade Act of 1974 as it affected TAA and Title III of JTPA. (As mentioned in chapter 1, the amendment to JTPA Title III is known as the Economic Dislocation and Worker Adjustment Assistance Act or EDWAA.) The 1988 TAA amendment continues the requirement that income-maintenance support is conditional on participation in an approved training program.

The LATA Program

Despite the arguments in the 1975 review resulting in the Australian government's decision to terminate SAA, the LATA initiative created in 1982 is also a categorical program which was initially directed at workers displaced from jobs in the steel industry. Since

1982, the program has been expanded to cover the coal mining industry in New South Wales, auto and auto parts manufacturers, and an International Harvester facility in Victoria. Workers displaced from their jobs in these industries are targeted for special assistance on the assumption that their displacement is especially likely to be the outcome of mass layoffs and plant closings. Large layoffs and plant closings present communities with the especially difficult problem of absorbing a large number of workers with similar skills who are all dumped on the local labor market at once.

The primary objective of the LATA program is to develop flexible training packages to meet the retraining needs of displaced workers, and there is no restriction placed on the course of study selected by trainees provided it is vocationally oriented. Training is provided in government or private educational institutions. In addition to covering the direct costs of classroom training, the LATA program supplies an income-maintenance allowance to trainees equal to what an individual would otherwise have received in UI benefits plus a supplementary adult training payment. Assistance is also provided to meet the costs of textbooks, equipment, and special course fees.

Heavy Engineering Labour Adjustment Assistance

This program is the labor market component of a broadly defined assistance package developed for the "heavy engineering" industry (i.e., the capital goods industry) by the Australian government. The other components include programs designed to assist industry employers in the areas of management efficiency, industrial development, and new product marketing.

As indicated in table 6.1, the labor market component of the heavy engineering industry assistance package includes four elements. Similar to the LATA program, the first funds formal training for up to 12 months for workers displaced from designated employers. In contrast to LATA, however, stronger emphasis is placed on the labor market relevance of the training curriculum selected. Eligible displaced workers also qualify for income-maintenance support.

The other three elements of the labor market program broaden substantially the scope of the services provided. The first of these appears to closely parallel the underlying philosophy of California's Employment Training Panel. That is, financial assistance is offered to encourage program-eligible employers to avoid layoffs by upgrading the skills of current employees through the establishment of formal training programs. Second, to encourage on-the-job training, displaced workers are made eligible for an employer wage-subsidy for up to six months. Finally, displaced workers who are unable to find suitable employment in their local labor markets, but who have firm job offers elsewhere, are eligible for relocation assistance.

The 1986 LATA Evaluation Study

As part of the LATA evaluation project carried out by the Australian Bureau of Labour Market Research, two surveys were administered to workers displaced from the General Motors-Holden (GMH) Acacia Ridge plant located in Brisbane. The first survey was conducted one month before the plant closed in October 1984, and the second was carried out eight months after the closure. A total of 445 GMH workers responded to both surveys. In many respects, these respondents closely resemble the auto workers surveyed in the Downriver project discussed in chapter 3. That is, the GMH workers are almost all males working in production jobs with families to support and considerable work experience. Average age and length of tenure for respondents are 42 years and 12 years, respectively.

LATA training courses available to GMH workers differed by type and length, and program participants were eligible to take as many different courses as they desired. Participants spent an average of 19 weeks on training. The main distinction between the types of courses taken is whether or not the course had to do with driver training (i.e., bus, train, or truck driving; forklift driving; operation of earth moving equipment; and light vehicle driving). During the 8- to 9-month observation period available for analysis, 31 percent of respondents chose to participate in one or more LATA training courses. About 54 percent of the courses involved driver training. The evaluation report by Ho-Trieu (1986) indicates that the probability of LATA participation peaks for workers in their mid-thirties. In addition, individuals with spouses in paid work and those who previously held supervisory or managerial positions are less likely to participate than other comparable workers.

The only labor market outcome variable examined by Ho-Trieu is job placement measured as full-time or part-time employment at the time of the follow-up interview. Net impact estimates are obtained by comparing the placement success of former GMH workers who chose to participate in LATA with the placement of those who chose not to participate. An obvious problem with this methodology is self-selection in the determination of program participation. A second problem is that the short length of the observation period implies that the net impact of longer training courses will be downwardly biased because of the reduced time available for job search. This source of bias was considered earlier in chapter 3 in the discussion of skill training in the Texas Worker Adjustment Demonstration projects. There the length of the observation period was 12 months.

With these caveats in mind, and recognizing also that the underlying parameter estimates have large standard errors, table 6.2 presents net impact estimates of LATA training holding constant the effects of age, marital status, number of children, and job search technique used (i.e., family, friends, and employment agencies; trade unions; newspapers; the Australian employment service; and direct employer contract). The partial probability estimates shown are calculated from the results of a logistic regression equation, and the estimates are interpreted as measuring changes in the probability that a typical former GMH worker will be reemployed by the end of the observation period. In the first column, consequently, a worker who took a training course of one to four weeks would have a placement probability 9 percentage points less than what his placement probability would have been had he opted not to undergo training. But if the short training course involves driver training, the net effect of LATA would be to increase the probability of reemployment by four percentage points ($= -9\% + 13\%$). The large negative estimate for courses longer than eight weeks is quite likely the result of the negative bias associated with a reduction in available job search time.

On the argument that it is not possible to accurately assess the impact of longer training courses, the second column of table 6.2

Table 6.2
Net Impact Estimates of LATA Training on the Probability
of Reemployment

Training variables	All participants	Excluding participants with longer training
Length of training:		
1–4 weeks	−9	⎫
		⎬ 0
5–8 weeks	−6	⎭
Longer than 8 weeks	−33	—
Driver training	13	9
Other training	—	−7

Source: Ho-Trieu (1986: tables 6.4 and 6.5).

Note: Other explanatory variables include age, marital status, number of children, and job search technique. In the second column, participants with total training of more than eight weeks are excluded from the regression, and training of eight weeks or less is treated as a continuous variable. — indicates that the variable is excluded from the regression.

reports probability estimates excluding LATA participants who took training courses exceeding eight weeks in total length. These results serve to emphasize the much larger impact of courses involving driver training relative to other LATA courses. Ho-Trieu (1986: 71–72) speculates that possible reasons for the strong impact of driver training include (1) a closer trainer-trainee relationship in driving courses, (2) the fact that driving skills can be learned independently of other factors such as English proficiency and basic academic skills, and (3) the greater opportunity offered those with driving qualifications for starting their own contracting businesses.

Summary

Described in this chapter are three programs funded by the Australian federal government to supply adjustment assistance services to displaced workers. The SAA program in effect from 1973 to 1976 is similar to the U.S. Trade Adjustment Assistance program in restricting program services to trade-displaced workers and in providing eligible workers with income-maintenance allowances. The other two programs—LATA and the Heavy Engineering Labour Adjustment Assistance program—provide income maintenance and skill training to workers displaced from a few selected industries. Both of these programs are still in operation.

Among the three Australian programs, only LATA has been subjected to program evaluation; and this evaluation is limited to a participant-nonparticipant comparison with the associated selection bias problem. The evaluation results reported indicate that the type of training provided (i.e., driver training) makes a substantial difference in the net impact analysis. In this respect, the LATA results reinforce a conclusion reached in chapter 3 for the Texas WAD projects. This conclusion is simply that training curriculums offered must match the interests and backgrounds of targeted workers to be effective.

7
Conclusion

This study examined evaluation evidence for nine different demonstration projects and operating programs on the labor market effectiveness of public retraining programs for displaced workers. Within the United States, quantitative results were presented in chapter 3 for four major, federally funded demonstration projects carried out during the 1980s. In chronological order, these are the Downriver program, the Buffalo program of the Dislocated Worker Demonstration Project, the Texas Worker Adjustment Demonstration, and the New Jersey UI Reemployment Demonstration. Although all four of the demonstrations have the common objective of evaluating alternative reemployment services including job search assistance, classroom training, and on-the-job training, they differ considerably in terms of geographic location, sample size, experimental design, and the target populations of displaced workers served. Turning from federal to state programs, examined in chapter 4 was the quantitative and qualitative evidence available for ongoing programs in California and Minnesota. California's Employment Training Panel funds skill training programs tailored to meet the needs of specific employers, while the Minnesota Employment and Economic Development program is a targeted wage-subsidy initiative designed to assist the growth of small businesses.

Beyond the borders of the U.S., evaluation evidence was discussed in chapters 5 and 6 for two Canadian programs and for an Australian program. The Canadian National Institutional Training Program provided displaced workers with classroom training, and the earlier Canadian Manpower Industrial Training Program program funded on-the-job training. The NITP is particularly noteworthy in that it supplied displaced workers with remedial education as well as skill training. Still in effect, Australia's Labour Adjustment Training Arrangements program targets CT services and income-maintenance allowances to workers displaced from selected industries including steel and coal mining.

Supplementing the evaluation evidence for these nine programs are net impact estimates obtained for three additional government programs not specifically designed to assist displaced workers. Considered in chapter 2 were the evaluations carried out for programs funded by CETA. In operation between 1973 and 1982, the broad-based CETA program went beyond assistance to displaced workers to include reemployment services and public-sector job creation directed toward disadvantaged workers and the cyclically unemployed. Included in the discussion of Minnesota's MEED program in chapter 4 were quantitative results from an evaluation study carried out for the Dayton targeted wage-subsidy experiment. Finally, evaluation evidence for the Canadian Youth Training Option was briefly considered in chapter 5 in connection with the CMITP program.

In this concluding chapter, I attempt to make sense of the net impact estimates and other evidence obtained for these projects and programs by first asking what these results have to say regarding the four policy questions posed in chapter 1. Then some suggestions are made regarding areas for further research.

Major Policy Questions

Question 1: Do some types of training work better than others?

Beginning with the evidence provided by the U.S. displaced worker demonstrations, the Buffalo, Texas WAD, and New Jersey projects indicate unambiguously that job search assistance strongly affects in the intended direction a variety of labor market outcomes, including earnings, placement and employment rates, and level of UI benefits. JSA allows for quick intervention before workers disperse after layoffs and plant closings; and, given its low cost per worker, the evidence suggests also that JSA services are cost effective. In view of the practical difficulties addressed in the New Jersey Demonstration of distinguishing early in the post-layoff period displaced workers from other unemployed workers, JSA's low cost offers the additional advantage of making it feasible to supply assistance even to those unemployed workers who turn out *ex post* to have little difficulty in locating new jobs or are recalled to their old jobs.

For the other major reemployment services, evidence gathered for all four U.S. demonstration projects indicates that classroom training fails to have a sizable incremental effect on earnings and employment above that of JSA-only. In particular, it certainly does not appear that the additional effect of classroom training is large enough to offset the higher cost of these services. The authors of the evaluation reports are plainly troubled by these unexpectedly weak results for CT, and they offer a number of qualifications to their findings. To anticipate the discussion of Question 4, these caveats include the following: (1) small sample sizes; (2) the problem that participants undergoing skill training have relatively little time left to receive placement assistance (given demonstration periods of fixed length); (3) the difficulty of finding training providers capable of putting together high-quality, short-duration training courses on short notice; and (4) the possibility that the classroom training provided is either not saleable in the local labor market or not of particular interest to targeted workers. Results obtained for the Australian LATA program reinforce the second caveat that net impact estimates for longer skill training programs may be downwardly biased due to the reduced length of time available for job search.

Regarding on-the-job training, it is interesting to note that the Secretary of Labor's Task Force on Economic Adjustment and Worker Dislocation (1986: 33–34) recommends that OJT rather than classroom training be regarded as the primary source of long-term skill upgrading for displaced workers. The CETA evaluations summarized in chapter 2 support this recommendation by showing generally larger net impact estimates for OJT than for CT. Among the four demonstration programs, the Buffalo project is the only one with enough participants placed in OJT slots to provide reasonably reliable estimates of the net impact of on-the-job training. Contrary to the CETA results, OJT fails to have a consistently positive effect on earnings. Nor does it have much of an impact on employment rates. Since OJT was primarily used in the Buffalo program as a placement tool, it appears that this service was of little value for program participants.

Although the evaluations of national Canadian and Australian retraining programs are not as methodologically rigorous, their findings regarding CT and OJT services support the generally negative findings yielded by the U.S. demonstrations. Using an externally selected comparison sample, skill training provided in a classroom setting is found in the Canadian NITP program not to significantly affect either weekly wages or annual earnings. In addition, the participant-non-participant comparison available for the Australian LATA program suggests that classroom training actually reduces the probability of re-employment during the observation period (although there is evidence that the training curriculum makes a difference). Similarly, the pre-program/post-program comparison available for program completers and dropouts for Canada's CMITP indicates that OJT had little impact on weekly wages. Given the present state of our knowledge, it seems reasonable to conclude, along with Bloom and Kulik (1986: 181), that skill training should be offered sparingly for well-specified needs and only where adequate local training resources are present.

Beyond the three major retraining services, the Basic Training for Skill Development (BTSD) component of the Canadian NITP is the only program discussed in this monograph that permits an examination of the labor market effectiveness of remedial education. Unfortunately, Canada's effort to upgrade basic mathematics and communications skills is found to significantly decrease both earnings and employment opportunities. There are at least two reasons, however, to expect these estimates to be downwardly biased. One is that BTSD training was not necessarily intended to prepare workers for immediate employment. The second reason is that the BTSD comparison group appears to be inappropriate since, in addition to being very small, it contains relatively few individuals with characteristics like those of trainees.

Question 2: Do some groups of workers benefit more from training than others?

The Texas WAD projects probably provide the best evidence of all of the demonstration projects and programs examined regarding differential program effects across workers classified by gender and race or ethnicity. In terms of earnings and employment, female participants in the El Paso WAD project are found to enjoy much larger net impact estimates than males in both the El Paso and Houston projects. More specifically, female participants in El Paso experienced a program-induced gain in annual earnings of $1,070 during the 1983–85 period; while the gains in annual earnings for men in Houston and El Paso were only $750 and $770, respectively. This difference between program sites is even more impressive when it is recognized that a majority of male Houston participants are white, whereas female El Paso participants are largely Hispanic.

Reinforcing the gender difference in the WAD results is evidence from the CETA evaluations and the Buffalo project indicating larger program effects for women than men. The Buffalo project also suggests that little difference in net impact estimates exists for blacks and whites, but that workers under age 45 benefit more from program services than do older workers.

Rather than race/ethnicity and sex differences, the results of the New Jersey Demonstration disaggregated by population subgroups emphasize the distinction between workers with marketable skills and workers facing long-term, structural reemployment problems. Clerical and other white-collar workers are examples of the former group, while blue-collar workers laid off from durable goods manufacturing jobs typify the latter. The evaluation report by Corson *et al.* (1989) indicates that program services were primarily of assistance to workers with marketable skills, a finding that is consistent with the New Jersey Demonstration's objective of encouraging rapid reemployment. As mentioned in chapter 1, however, a case can be made that it is the sizable minority of displaced workers who are at risk of lengthy spells of joblessness to whom adjustment assistance should be targeted. These individuals are likely to require longer-run, more intensive services.

Question 3: To the extent that training improves reemployment prospects, does it work by increasing post-training wage rates or by reducing the duration of unemployment?

For all program services combined, the Buffalo project permits the calculation of short-run program effects on weekly hours and average weekly earnings. The larger percentage effect on average weekly earnings than weekly hours suggests that the Buffalo program boosted hourly wages for those reemployed during the first six post-program months. Buttressing this finding, an analysis of state administrative data indicates for the New Jersey Demonstration that each of the three program treatments (i.e., JSA-only, JSA plus retraining, and JSA plus a reemployment bonus) had a small positive impact on the wages of reemployed workers.

In contrast, the more detailed quarter-by-quarter program impact estimates calculated for the Texas WAD projects and the New Jersey Demonstration indicate that this short-run positive effect on wage rates does not persist over time. For both men and women, the time pattern of the WAD results shows that the program increased quarterly earnings in the first and second quarters, followed by gradually decaying impacts for subsequent quarters. Similar results broken down by program treatment are obtained using follow-up interview data on employment and earnings in the New Jersey project. Thus, while the reemployment process was speeded up by program services in both demonstrations, participants' employment opportunities appear ultimately to be no better and their wages no higher than those of the members of the control group. There is little convincing evidence, in other words, that program services in either the Texas WAD or the New Jersey Demonstration increased labor productivity. The evaluation of on-the-job training in the Canadian CMITP also suggests, as noted, that program completion had little impact in terms of wage gains.

Question 4: Referring specifically to vocational training, how do we know what to train workers to do?

An important contribution of the displaced worker demonstration projects is to make apparent the difficulty in a short-duration demonstration of designing solid training curricula that meet the market test of providing saleable skills. Of the four U.S. demonstrations, Downriver program planners probably paid the most attention to the problem of providing retraining in occupations expected to be in high demand. Yet, as described in chapter 3 and noted earlier, skill training is not found to have significantly improved Downriver participants' reemployment prospects above the assistance provided by JSA. Corson, Maynard, and Wichita (1984: 16) note for all six sites of the Dislocated Worker Demonstration Project that key lessons learned are that (1) many displaced workers will not be able to adapt to classroom training, and (2) despite attempts to base course selection on labor market data, many successful program graduates may not be able to locate training-related jobs. These authors go on to recommend the use of performance-based contracting with training vendors as one way to improve participant screening in determining access to CT programs and to increase post-program placement and job retention rates. The WAD demonstration also emphasizes that one reason for low program take-up rates and modest net impact estimates is that CT curricula may not match the backgrounds and perceived needs of client workers. Evaluation results obtained for the Australian LATA program underscore the point that the type of training provided can make a substantial difference in net impact estimates.

State-funded retraining programs are typically more tailored to meet the needs of individual employers than federal programs, and chapter 4 focused attention on employer involvement in California's ETP and the program's stringent performance standards. California employers are encouraged to propose individual retraining projects for ETP funding. If a project is approved and a contract negotiated, the employer selects trainees according to its own specification, sets standards for successful program completion, and approves the training curriculum if an outside training provider is used. ETP's performance standards permit training providers to be reimbursed for training expenses only for those trainees who successfully complete the program and are placed in training-related jobs at stipulated wages and are retained in those jobs for at least 90 days.

Allowing employers to participate in trainee selection and the use of performance-based contracting clearly should contribute to strong program performance in terms of job placement, and preliminary empirical results obtained for ETP indicate a sizable program effect on annual earnings. Although it is a training initiative directed at noncollege-bound youth rather than displaced workers, the evaluation of the Canadian YTO program provides additional evidence that the involvement of private-sector employers in a combined CT-OJT program can make a substantial difference in the post-program employability of participants. Nevertheless, the ETP approach has been subjected to a number of criticisms. One of these is that program performance standards increase the likelihood that training providers will select those eligible workers least in need of retraining. A second criticism centers on the strong incentive given employers to retrain current employees, as opposed to offering training to unemployed workers. A consequence of the observed increase over time in the retraining of the employed is that ETP may be substituting public funds for the training investments employers would have made themselves in the program's absence.

In the context of these criticisms, an important outcome of Minnesota's MEED wage-subsidy program is its demonstration that it is possible to target assistance to the hard-to-employ and still enjoy widespread business support, particularly the support of small businessmen. That is, Minnesota program officials appear to have successfully overcome the stigma associated by employers with program vouchers in the Dayton targeted wage-subsidy experiment. The internal evaluation of Canada's CMITP program reinforces the MEED evidence in indicating that small employers have a substantially greater propensity than larger employers to participate in retraining initiatives directed at unemployed workers. On the other hand, large Canadian employers, like large California employers, are disproportionately likely to participate in programs intended to upgrade the skills of existing employees. The CMITP employer survey data also suggest that among participating employers, it is small firms that are most likely to respond to a wage-subsidy program by generating a net increase in the delivery of training services.

Agenda for Future Research

The recommendation that emerges most strongly from the empirical evidence analyzed in this monograph is that JSA should be the core service on the menu of adjustment assistance services offered displaced workers. With respect to other services, however, the evidence is not as conclusive; and there appear to be several topics on which future research is needed. Important items on the agenda for future research include the following.

1. It is reasonable to conclude that, if offered at all, skill training provided in a classroom setting should be limited to carefully screened trainees whose specific needs can be adequately matched with local training resources. But even in this highly controlled situation, as noted by Bloom and Kulik (1986: 182), whether a high quality, targeted skill training program can be cost effective is an open question and should be the subject of further research.

2. A closely related issue is the recommendation of the Secretary of Labor's Task Force (1986: 34) that classroom training be matched to the needs of identified employers and that contracts with training providers be performance-based. A clear benefit of placing these constraints on the design of CT programs is the associated increase in job placement. Nevertheless, this benefit needs to be carefully weighed against the potential costs of creaming in the trainee selection process and of providing a windfall to employers who would have otherwise supplied retraining at their own expense. Further research, perhaps building on the experience of California's ETP, on how to design CT programs to minimize these costs would be helpful.

3. The Secretary of Labor's Task Force (1986: 34) also strongly recommends that OJT, as opposed to CT, be the preferred method of long-term skill training. Yet, the limited empirical evidence reviewed here suggests, at best, a lukewarm assessment of the effectiveness of on-the-job training. A key issue in the design of OJT programs involves the incentives necessary to stimulate employer interest in providing retraining opportunities; and further examination of programs, like Minnesota's MEED, which appear to be well received by employers, would be of value.

4. Many studies of the reemployment assistance needs of displaced workers include a recommendation that strengthening basic skills is essential to allow workers to cope with rapid technological change and increased international competitiveness (see, for example, Cyert and Mowery 1987: 185–86 and the Secretary of Labor's Task Force 1986: 33–34). Despite the suggestion in the Corson *et al.* (1989) evaluation of the New Jersey Demonstration that remedial education

may be needed for displaced workers who face long-term, structural reemployment problems, only the Canadian NITP of the programs examined here furnishes quantitative evidence on the effectiveness of this program service. The negative results of the Robinson *et al.* (1985) evaluation of NITP's remedial education component must be interpreted recognizing the caveats noted earlier in this chapter. An important topic for further research is identification of the proper objective function for remedial training programs, followed by additional evaluation evidence on the determinants of success and failure of these programs.

References

Ashenfelter, Orley. "Estimating the Effect of Training Programs on Earnings," *Review of Economics and Statistics* 60 (February 1978): 47–57.

Barnow, Burt S. "The Impact of CETA Programs on Earnings: A Review of the Literature," *Journal of Human Resources* 22 (Spring 1987): 157–93.

Bassi, Laurie J. "The Effect of CETA on the Postprogram Earnings of Participants," *Journal of Human Resources* 18 (Fall 1983): 539–56.

Bednarzik, Robert W., and James A. Orr. "The Effectiveness of Trade-Related Worker Adjustment Policies in the United States," Economic Discussion Paper 15, Bureau of International Labor Affairs, U.S. Department of Labor (February 1984).

Bishop, John H., and Mark Montgomery. "Evidence on Firm Participation in Employment Subsidy Programs," *Industrial Relations* 25 (Winter 1986): 56–64.

Bloom, Howard S., and Jane Kulik. "Evaluation of the Worker Adjustment Demonstration: Final Report." Abt Associates (July 1986).

Bloom, Howard S., and Maureen A. McLaughlin. "CETA Training Programs—Do They Work for Adults?" Joint CBO-NCEP Report (1982).

Brown, Charles, and James Medoff. "The Employer Size-Wage Effect," *Journal of Political Economy* 97 (October 1989): 1027–59.

Bureau of Labour Market Research. *Structural Change and the Labour Market.* Research Report No. 11. Canberra: Australian Government Publishing Service, 1987.

Burtless, Gary. "Are Targeted Wage Subsidies Harmful? Evidence from a Wage Voucher Experiment," *Industrial and Labor Relations Review* 39 (October 1985): 105–14.

Corson, Walter, and Walter Nicholson. "Trade Adjustment Assistance for Workers: Results of a Survey of Recipients Under the Trade Act of 1974," in *Research In Labor Economics,* edited by Ronald G. Ehrenberg. Greenwich, CT: JAI Press, 1981.

Corson, Walter, Rebecca Maynard, and Jack Wichita. "Process and Implementation Issues In the Design and Conduct of Programs to Aid the Reemployment of Dislocated Workers," Mathematica Policy Research (October 30, 1984).

Corson, Walter, Sharon Long, and Rebecca Maynard. "An Impact Evaluation of the Buffalo Dislocated Worker Demonstration Program," Mathematica Policy Research (March 12, 1985).

Corson, Walter, and Stuart Kerachsky. "The New Jersey Unemployment Insurance Reemployment Demonstration Project: Interim Report." Employment and Training Administration, U.S. Department of Labor (1987).

Corson, Walter, Shari Dunstan, Paul Decker, and Anne Gordon. "New Jersey Unemployment Insurance Reemployment Demonstration Project." Unemployment Insurance Occasional Paper 89–3. Employment and Training Administration, U.S. Department of Labor (1989).

Cyert, Richard M., and David C. Mowery, eds. *Technology and Employment: Innovation and Growth in the U.S. Economy.* Washington, DC: National Academy Press, 1987.

Dickinson, Katherine P., Terry R. Johnson, and Richard W. West. "An Analysis of the Impact of CETA Programs on Participants' Earnings," *Journal of Human Resources* 21 (Winter 1986): 64–91.

Employment and Immigration Canada, Canadian Jobs Strategy Group. "The Canadian Jobs Strategy: A Review." (July 1988).

———. Program Evaluation Branch. "Evaluation of the Canada Manpower Industrial Training Program." (April 1981).

———. Program Evaluation Branch. "Evaluation of the Youth Training Option." (February 1987).

———. Public Affairs and Strategic Policy and Planning. "Success In the Works: A Policy Paper." (August 4, 1989).

Employment Training Panel. "Annual Report 1985." (1985).

———. "Report to the Legislature, 1987." (1987).

———. "Report to the Legislature, 1988" (November 1988).

Finifter, David H. "An Approach to Estimating Net Earnings Impact of Federally Subsidized Employment and Training Programs," *Evaluation Review* 11 (August 1987): 528–47.

Flaim, Paul O., and Ellen Sehgal. "Displaced Workers of 1979–83: How Well Have They Fared?" *Monthly Labor Review* 108 (June 1985): 3–16.

Fraker, Thomas, and Rebecca Maynard. "The Adequacy of Comparison Group Designs for Evaluations of Employment-Related Programs," *Journal of Human Resources* 22 (Spring 1987): 194–227.

Geraci, Vincent J. "Short-Term Indicators of Job Training Program Effects on Long-Term Participant Earnings." Report prepared for the U.S. Department of Labor under Contract No. 20–48–82–16 (1984).

Heckman, James J., V. Joseph Hotz, and Marcelo Dabos. "Do We Need Experimental Data to Evaluate the Impact of Manpower Training on Earnings?" *Evaluation Review* 11 (August 1987): 395–427.

Ho-Trieu, Ngoc Luan. "Factors Associated with Retrenched Workers' Participation In LATA and Their Re-employment Prospects." Department of Employment and Industrial Relations. Canberra (June 1986).

Kletzer, Lori Gladstein. "Returns to Seniority After Permanent Job Loss," *American Economic Review* 79 (June 1989): 536–43.

Kulik, Jane, D. Alton Smith, and Ernst W. Stromsdorfer. "The Downriver Community Conference Economic Readjustment Program: Final Evaluation Report." Abt Associates (May 18, 1984).

Kuttner, Robert. "Getting Off the Dole," *The Atlantic Monthly* (September 1985): 74–79.

LaLond, Robert J. "Evaluating the Econometric Evaluations of Training Programs with Experimental Data," *American Economic Review* 76 (September 1986): 604–20.

Leigh, Duane E. *Assisting Displaced Workers: Do the States Have a Better Idea?* Kalamazoo, MI: W. E. Upjohn Institute, 1989.

Levitan, Sar A., and Frank Gallo. *A Second Chance: Training for Jobs.* Kalamazoo, MI: W. E. Upjohn Institute, 1988.

Minnesota Department of Jobs and Training. *Minnesota Employment and Economic Development (MEED) Wage Subsidy Program, July 1985–December 1986.* (1987).

Moore, Richard W., Wellford W. Wilms, and Roger E. Bolus. "Training for Change: An Analysis of the Outcomes of California Employment Training Panel Programs." Training Research Corporation (January 19, 1988).

Neumann, George R. "The Labor Market Adjustments of Trade Displaced Workers: The Evidence from the Trade Adjustment Assistance Program," in *Research In Labor Economics,* edited by Ronald G. Ehrenberg. Greenwich, CT: JAI Press, 1978.

Office of Technology Assessment. *Technology and Structural Unemployment: Reemploying Displaced Adults.* Washington, DC: Congress of the United States, 1986.

O'Neill, Dave M. "Employment Tax Credit Programs: The Effects of Socioeconomic Targeting Provisions," *Journal of Human Resources* 17 (Summer 1982): 449–59.

Podgursky, Michael, and Paul Swaim. "Duration of Joblessness Following Displacement," *Industrial Relations* 26 (Fall 1987a): 213–26.

———— and ————. "Job Displacement and Earnings Loss: Evidence from the Displaced Worker Survey," *Industrial and Labor Relations Review* 41 (October 1987b): 17–29.

Rangan, Asha. "MEED Works: A Look at Minnesota's Investment In People, Jobs and Communities." The Jobs Now Coalition (March 1985).

Robinson, R. B., S. E. Varette, D. A. Smith, H. K. Vodden, and R. E. Eaton. "Evaluation—National Institutional Training Program (NITP): Final Report." Abt Associates of Canada (June 1985).

Rode, Peter. "MEED Means More Business: Job Growth through Minnesota's Wage Subsidy Program." The Jobs Now Coalition (March 1988).

Secretary of Labor's Task Force on Economic Adjustment and Worker Dislocation. "Economic Adjustment and Worker Dislocation in a Competitive Society." (December 1986).

Simpson, Wayne. "An Econometric Analysis of Industrial Training In Canada," *Journal of Human Resources* 19 (Fall 1984): 435–51.

Stevens, David. "State Industry-Specific Training Programs: 1986" University of Missouri-Columbia (December 1986).

Westat. "Continuous Longitudinal Manpower Survey Net Impact Report No. 1: Impact on 1977 Earnings of New FY 1976 CETA Enrollees In Selected Program Activities." Report prepared for the U.S. Department of Labor under Contract No. 23–24–75–07 (1981).

Woodbury, Stephen A., and Robert G. Spiegelman. "Bonuses to Workers and Employers to Reduce Unemployment: Randomized Trials In Illinois," *American Economic Review* 77 (September 1987): 513–30.

INDEX

115